THE TOP PERFORMER

Practical guide to being a consistent top performer and defying the lay off!

PRASHANT DIXIT

INDIA • SINGAPORE • MALAYSIA

Notion Press

No.8, 3rd Cross Street
CIT Colony, Mylapore
Chennai, Tamil Nadu – 600004

First Published by Notion Press 2021
Copyright © Prashant Dixit 2021
All Rights Reserved.

ISBN
Hardcase: 978-1-63806-649-1
Paperback: 978-1-63806-574-6

This book has been published with all efforts taken to make the material error-free after the consent of the author. However, the author and the publisher do not assume and hereby disclaim any liability to any party for any loss, damage, or disruption caused by errors or omissions, whether such errors or omissions result from negligence, accident, or any other cause.

While every effort has been made to avoid any mistake or omission, this publication is being sold on the condition and understanding that neither the author nor the publishers or printers would be liable in any manner to any person by reason of any mistake or omission in this publication or for any action taken or omitted to be taken or advice rendered or accepted on the basis of this work. For any defect in printing or binding the publishers will be liable only to replace the defective copy by another copy of this work then available.

This book is dedicated to my family, friends, managers, colleagues, team members and their families.....!

If it wasn't for you – this book would have never been ☺

CONTENTS

Thanks!		7
Note		9
Telephone Rings and......		11
Introduction		15
Gratitude & Thanks to...		25
Chapter 1	Knowledge	29
Chapter 2	Attitude	46
Chapter 3	Communication Skills	79
Chapter 4	Documentation	91
Chapter 5	Upward Management	97
Chapter 6	Downward Management	118
Chapter 7	Ensuring Employability	140
Chapter 8	Interviews	148
Chapter 9	Social Media Management	159
Chapter 10	Professional Networking	163

Chapter 11   Exits   166

Chapter 12   Job is not life   170

Note for readers   175

Appendix 1   177

Appendix 2 – Extra Stuff   179

Appendix 3 – Research Details   180

Appendix 4   184

THANKS!

You win a smile

You have contributed to happiness of some unfortunate kids and elderly people.

100% of the earnings of this book will be donated.

This book is a small gift from you and I to the unfortunate disowned kids and parents, this is just to say thanks to God for all what he has given to all of us!

A. **Kids:** *The unfortunate ones who haven't had a chance to be under the nurturing shade of parents. Don't have anyone whom they can call father or mother.*

B. **Parents:** *Who are struggling alone in their old age. In some cases their kids felt they don't need them anymore and in some cases – we just don't know.*

** *Money will be distributed to orphanage and old age homes. Like Sofos (Pune) & Siddhi Vrudha Ashram (Pune)*

NOTE

In case you need any guidance, support or interested in personal coaching with Prashant and his team please connect with us at

Email: prashant.dixit.win@gmail.com

Facebook: prashant.dixit.win

Twitter: @prashant_dixit_

Instagram: @iprashantdixit

Website: www.prashantdixit.in

TELEPHONE RINGS AND......

I am experiencing such panic for the first time. Reluctant to take this call. I and my manager Adarsh sit across the table where this phone is ringing.

I muster all the courage I could and press the handsfree button - while my eyes still fixed at the wall where Abhay is smiling at me from the team photograph. This photograph was taken last year during our yearly event.

"Hello Prashant" crackles. Abhay's (name changed) voice happy and excited made me feel even worse. I missed a heartbeat.

"Hello Abhay, I have Adarsh and Ritu (name changed) from HR with me.

Abhay shocked and speechless with the unexpected people on call.

"Hi Everyone, Prashant - do you want me to call you later, we can reschedule this *one on one* meeting, if you are busy" - still unaware that the agenda of this call has changed long back.

"No Abhay, the team here is for a purpose, I would like to share"

Due to recent business realignment your position has become redundant.

"Your full & final will be settled by the HR Team. Your services are no longer required"

Abhay broke down, cried for a few seconds followed by a few moments of anger and frustration and finally helplessness took over. He went silent. Once HR completed her briefing - Abhay just said thanks and walked out of the room. He didn't disconnect so we could hear him walk out and thud of the door.

Life had changed that day for him and myself. I couldn't get over the pain of firing for some time. It was my first time into such conversation while he and his family was shocked & despaired.

I have unfortunately been on such conversations for couple of times now – at times due to organizations need, at times performance of individual and at times the attitude. I can assure you, words don't matter - how much you may try to soften the blow - these words "you are fired" always strike as a thunderbolt…

On the brighter side - thankfully I have been opportune enough to distribute several promotion and increment letters as well. In a few instances people have come back with welled-up eyes and said BIG THANK YOU for making this happen.

We just observed two opposite situations but the important ones

1. In which person is fired
2. In which person is awarded/rewarded

What do you think, is it a matter of luck, favouritism, nepotism, politics or planned efforts that determines your fate in an organization?

Most of the people who were fired did not have any early warnings – "You are fired" news was delivered as an unexpected surprise.

Are you sure no one is evaluating your name for the next list?

Idea is not to scare you but its the harsh reality of business today.

There are 2 things in Business

A. Liabilities

B. Assets.

Orgs are trying to cut the slack and let go the liabilities while paying extra money and growth to retain and increase their Assets.

Question

Are you an Asset or a gradually growing liability?

What lies ahead of you in next few weeks, months and year?

INTRODUCTION

We realize we need to be an asset to get any kind of growth, those promotions, salary hikes etc.

This book is a guide to become one!

Not just an Asset but a performing asset. The top performing one. Be a -

"The Top Performer"

Now who can help or give an advice? Someone who has gone this route. Who has been part of the process. In the process there are 2 main participants – 1. Employee who is being evaluated and 2. Manager/Leader who is evaluating. Thus this book presents all what you need to do as an employee and this also shares what matters to managers.

Each manager will be different from other, they would have different personality type, preferences and challenges – so how do we know what will work with your manager (or devil ☺ - given jokes on bosses)?

To answer that question – I reached out to some senior leaders and friends who have been doing performance evaluation for years now. I wanted to establish what attributes did matter to them?

Introduction

In the process we collected experience that if added, sums up to 325 years of total experience and 200+ years of people management to provide you the guidance.

These numbers were ridiculous but on a second thought it made sense – as 2 people share summary of 5 years of their experience – they both get benefit of 5 years of the other person's experience. With the same analogy – We couldn't have learned so much by our own experience and thus learning from other's experience does count. *(Check Appendix 3 for research details).*

This book is written to help and guide and thus I insist to not to blindly believe - think about what is mentioned and validate it with examples around you, your experiences - if you feel it resonates with you and your observations - give it a chance and try to adopt and in case it doesn't matches with your observations & experience - feel free to park or let go those ideas - there is rarely one way to success - everyone leaves their own trail - what we have to try is to learn from the mistakes / shortcomings / experience of others as well to avoid the obvious pitfalls and make your journey smoother and faster.

"There is no fun in falling in each pit to learn there was a pit, learn from those who have already passed that road"

– Prashant

How do I qualify to be a guide?

Early in my career I was a poor performer myself and then turned it around to be a consistent top performer. There was a continuous change in my Organizations, work, technology, role and most interestingly managers. In spite of all these changes – I have grown consistently.

At times some people believe

Introduction

"Boss Favourite" becomes → "Top Performer".

However its other way round the

"Top Performers" become → "Boss Favourite"

I have worked for 20 managers in 14 years, roughly 1.4 manager a year so I can tell you with reasonable certainty that the success cannot be just achieved if you manage to get "favourite" of one boss. As in my example nepotism, favouritism and other "isms" are out of window as I really didn't had enough time to play favourite neither they had enough tenure with me to pull me through all the ranks even if they liked me.

This turnaround has to be built brick by brick with planning, smart and hard work simultaneously. *For more details on this turnaround story please refer to Appendix 4.*

Why even the effort to read this book? I wrote this book because of the pain. I have witnessed very closely the plight of people who are fired. I have seen very closely what happens when in spite of all your hard work you are not given what you believe you earnestly deserve. Someone else was promoted above you just because of some weird reason. I have observed the pain of people not having enough time or money in spite of working very hard, distress/stress of long working hours, feeling of failure and being considered as a waste while you have given all your heart and soul to make something work. After seeing the plight of many colleagues and friends and realizing that no good help is available for even who want to learn the trade secret, I chose to collate the best practises that can bring meaning to life that can help people to restore work-life balance, get acknowledged or recognised for their work. This book will help you build a very strong foundation towards a successful career. It would ensure that you retain your job in spite of all the problems in the industry and also get hikes or pay corrections whenever they happen. The idea here is to be the first one to get advantage of anything and everything that the organisation has to offer. Right now you are holding in your hands a great compilation of fail proof time tested techniques and methods that would position you at the top of your organisation.

Before we get any further, please note this book is curated for folks who are starting their career and less than 7 years of work ex. In case you have spent more than 7 years in the job – you would mostly know this out of your experience but you are welcome to check your experience against 200+ years of people management!

Why not be a happy mediocre? Why a TOP Performer?

The top performer is not a matter of chance it's a matter of hard work, it's a matter of strategy, it's a matter of planned efforts towards achieving that objective of being a top performer. Most of us believe that we have to be a top performer but few understand the "why" of it. Why be a top performer? Why to be part of the top 10 category of the infamous bell curve. In order to understand this lets evaluate the perks of top performers. First of all - the salary increase. Everyone in the office works for almost the same amount of hours but one person gets 10% to 20% better hike while the other person gets 5%. For someone these numbers may be just 5% and 10% but if you look at it - Its double.

For same hours spent away from family you are earning half of the other person - Isn't it sad & bad?

The salary hike that you lose is just a small thing. You are losing much more. You may be skipped for a promotion and that person is already a level up while you slogged - equally. Next time let's say the promotion happens for both of you but he/she would still be ahead of you. Any opportunity loss, any step where you fail to get promoted any step where you fail to get a hike, any step where you do not get a good project or job in your current organisation, you are losing and that loss counts!!

What is a solution? How can we ensure that we are not missing out on important opportunities?

Put this book to use. Dive in and follow the suggestions & recommendations advised.

This is an important call for action if you don't act now you may loose on the next upcoming opportunity. You might be a few months away from next hike discussion, next promotion, next performance review, so the **time** *is now. Start building it up right away.*

Let's start – wishing you an unstoppable success!!

Let's set the engine roaring, make a loud noise – Announce

YOU ARE ARRIVING!

Love & Wishes
Prashant Dixit

Research with Leaders across various Organization some listed below.

Cumulative **People Management Experience** of these Leaders 200+ Years

GRATITUDE & THANKS TO...

I have been in corporate for around 1.5 decades and continue to learn and grow. I acknowledge that I have been opportune to work for some of the world's most prestigious organisations and this journey has been remarkable.

Thanks to excellent colleagues, leaders, project managers, customers and other remarkable people who met on the way on this journey. Each one of them contributed in one way or the other. This book is a product or a sculpture which has been shaped by the influence of some of the best minds in business. I take pride that I have been associated with some of the best people you can ever get a chance to work with. This book is only a small reflection of uncountable learnings that came my way on this journey. Thanks to each one of you!

Special Thanks to Leaders who spared time and efforts to share their insights.

Gratitude & Thanks to…

Name	Org	Designation
Mr Adarsh Mudugere	VMware	Director
Mr Ajay Sharma	Cisco	Services Delivery Manager
Mr Ambrish Sharma	Cisco Systems	Services Delivery Manager
Mr Anantha Amancharla	SS&C	Director
Mr Anurag Bahadur	Cisco	Senior Director
Mr Gerald Wilson	Vodafone Idea	Vice President
Mr Krishna Pandey	NICE	Director
Mr Madhup Nagpal	Druva	Vice President
Mr Matthew Stramel	Zscaler	Senior Director
Mr Murali Nayak	Veritas Technologies	Director
Mr Ravi Mylariah	Teknodreams software	Vice President
Mr Sameer Bondre	Kohler	Director
Mr Sameer Srivastava	Mytel	Director
Mr Uttam Banerjee	Ekam Eco Solutions	CEO
Mr Wasi Abidi	Mondelz international	Global Head Delivery(DWP)

Special thanks to **Sameer Srivastava** – Who actually provided the idea that helped me do the research more effectively & efficiently.

Feedback is the most crucial part of anyone's growth and same holds true for the book. I am thankful to my friends – Pranav Jha, Nicky Jha, Baljit Randhawa, Divya Dixit for taking out time to read and share the feedback.

Divya really hit it hard, she didn't shy calling out all what didn't feel right. There were many changes brought in due to her and Pranav's inputs. Thanks folks!

That's what true friends are all about.

One person who has been the biggest support throughout the journey – my dear wife Shweta! Words always fall short to convey all what you mean to me. This would have taken a decade to hit the print if you would have not compiled, proof read and made the necessary changes.

Last but not the least my cute little world ☺

Parents:

Mr Pradeep Dixit, Mr Harish Yogi, Mrs Madhulika Dixit, Mrs Uma Yogi, Mr Arun Dixit, Mrs Meenakshi Dixit, Mrs Nalin

Siblings:

Ajit Tiwari, Kshitij Yogi, Sandhya Yogi, Mayuri Tiwari, Samarth Dixit, Srishti Dixit, Siddhant Dixit

Kids:

Aarna, Araina, Adrika, Amayra

Lots of love and gratitude!

Chapter 1

KNOWLEDGE

स्व गृहे पूज्यते पिथरा, स्व ग्रामे पूज्यते प्रभु, स्व देशे पूज्यते राजा, विद्वान सर्वत्र पूज्यते!!!

Swa gruhe Poojyathe Pithara, Swa graame Poojyathe Prabhu, Swa deshe Poojyathe Raja, Vidhwan Sarvathra Poojyathe!!!

Means:

Swagruhe (In own House) Parents are respected, Swagraam (In own village) A landlord or a rich man is respected. Swadeshe (in own kingdom) the king is respected and adored. But a Vidhwan (a scholar) is respected and adored all over the world.

This holds good in corporate as well. The first and foremost building block of your career, the basic pillar of your success is knowledge and it is non-negotiable. You just cannot negotiate anything for knowledge.

"Knowledge is Power" we have heard this many times but it's actually the "Applied Knowledge" which is power. In case you don't have knowledge or you have knowledge but you don't act with that knowledge - it's one of the same thing, its worthless. Thus we will focus on two aspects of knowledge:

1. Accumulating Knowledge
2. Putting this Accumulated knowledge into action

When it comes to your job performance - which knowledge is important? There are two aspects to it

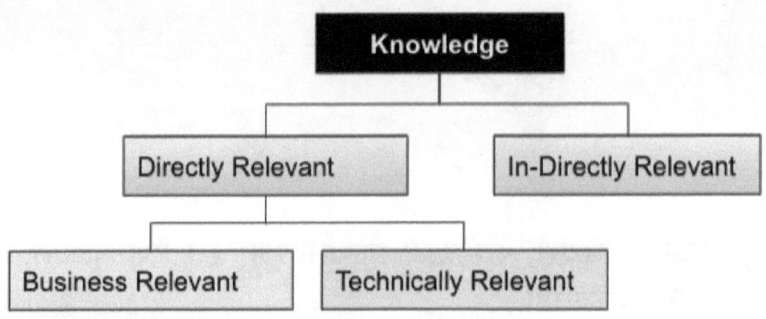

A. Directly Relevant

Function Relevant Business and Technical Knowledge.

B. Indirectly Relevant

Every Information/Data/Knowledge other than Direct Knowledge. This is also significant as it helps gaining Direct Knowledge. Let's review them but may not focus too much in this book.

Very Basic Example: Let's say you are working with a customer or boss who is IPL or FIFA fan and you happen to be knowledgeable about the same - It can help you strike the right chords due to association.

Another example: You are well versed with Geography and History this can be helpful while working on the projects those are global in nature and spread across various geo locations.

Now, let's assume we understand, Indirect Knowledge is good to have but the Direct Knowledge is *sine qua non* – the must have.

Directly relevant Knowledge is a sum total of two sub aspects:

1. Business aspect and
2. Technical aspects

Now, the question is how do we learn and accumulate this knowledge and where is the starting line? The answer is:

"The more you know, the more you know how little you know"

When you learn one thing it opens up or leads to other dimensions those were not visible to you earlier. When you learn, you climb up the ladder and with each rising step your view expands, you get more visibility to the opportunities of learning that lay dormant earlier.

"People who move mountains start by moving small rocks and stones"

similarly - we shall start from our day to day activities.

Here is the trick:

Today or Tomorrow - Whenever you are in office and you pick up your day job - Start questioning!

Let's say your day job is to do a monitoring. Do a quiz for yourself -

- What do I actually monitor?
- What is the business outcome for which Organization is spending on me to monitor this thing?
- What is in the backend that is pushing this feed that I monitor?
- What different actions are taken by the next team to whom I pass on the information to

These are few questions but the list can run into pages - depending on how sincerely you want to learn. This is a fission reaction. It will transform your level of knowledge and your standing within your team.

Another example - In case someone is in TESTING/Development. The person should question himself:

- What are you TESTING and WHY?
- What business impact/advantage your code delivers?
- Why is it so important for businesses to have this code?
- What losses business may incur if code fails?
- How this would integrate with the larger codes running already in the system?

When you ask such questions you gradually start getting deeper insights into what you do and this helps you to assimilate the direct knowledge. Learning is not a one-time activity - it has to be done regularly. Like we need basic hygiene and food daily similarly - every day we need to learn - may be some days you would have a light meal and other days a gluttonous party. All the individuals who learn with time, invest efforts in learning become outstandingly brilliant in their domains. You can talk to them Inside Out about their topic of expertise and you would be impressed that they have learnt it from all the possible means.

Let me share an experience, I joined CISCO and there I met two excellent technical resource Manoj Raju and Ankit Pandey - They were supposed to ideally know only one Setup (Contact Centre or Unified Communication) but gentlemen were so profound that they were equally helpful in all the three functions within the team - Contact Centre (CC), Unified Communication(UC) and Interactive Voice Response(IVR). This reinforced my believe that once you are sound with the basics - you can be helpful in more than one way - This expertise is difficult to master but has very rewarding proposition. It was no wonder that both of them enjoyed great respect within customers and Cisco fraternity.

Similarly lot of my friends who were technically outstanding, have been a consistent performer, rose up the ranks from being Engineer to Technical Manager to Operations Manager to Functional head in much less time when compared to folks who were not that Knowledgeable. There are several such examples who took their career as a sprint and made a great career.

When you are knowledgeable you automatically generate a lot of respect for yourself and this respect is not just because you know things but you are able to apply. This knowledge helps bail out team from problems which creates a certain amount of positive dependency on you.

I have been into many situations during escalations where I feel if I could just reach these guys the problem would stand resolved immediately. Such criticality once established, people are longing to get you on call as they know your presence will make a lot of difference to the given situation. That's where you earn the respect, dependency and reputation which is necessary for being an outstanding performer.

Now, if you were a manager of such person - what kind of treatment, promotion or hike you would reward to this person when compared to other team members who are just pushing the cart?

Salary, Hike, Promotions, Flexibility and Appreciations flow to them effortlessly. In order to have all of this very first step it to be *Knowledgeable*.

Now, when we embark on the journey of being knowledgeable and hence the performer: there are two asks

1. Know the grain
2. Go Against the grain

Let's take them one at a time:

1. **Know the grain:** Having an end to end awareness of your business from various interdependent perspectives. Maybe your job is to develop a small code but you must know how it integrates in the big picture. For example - You do a code and have 4 team dependent on your code. You must really understand HOW do these teams get impacted through your work. Then you will have a more holistic perspective and better decision making.

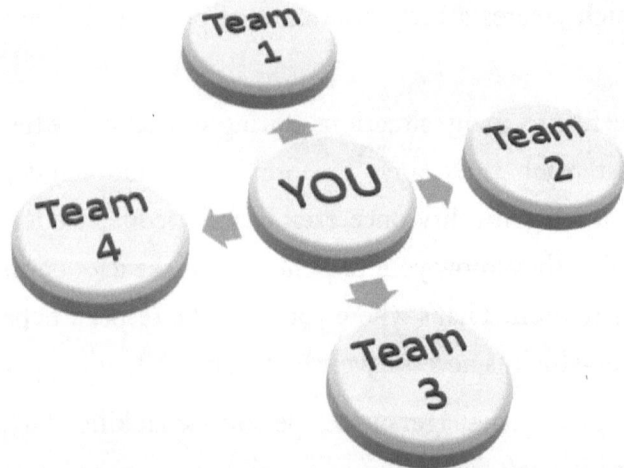

2. **Go Against the grain:** Once you know what you do and how it impacts your downstream and upstream teams you can start finding better ways to integrate and deliver.

Use **Dependency Diagram**. In this you make your process in a box and list down all the associated process those happen before your process kicks in and similarly what happens post completion of your own process. Let's assume you do Process 3 as per the below diagram, then you must surely know Process 2 and process 4 - Even better if you know all process from 1 to 5 because this understanding enables you for better decision making and you would have enough details & facts to assert your point within and outside your team.

This is one of the most important trick!:)

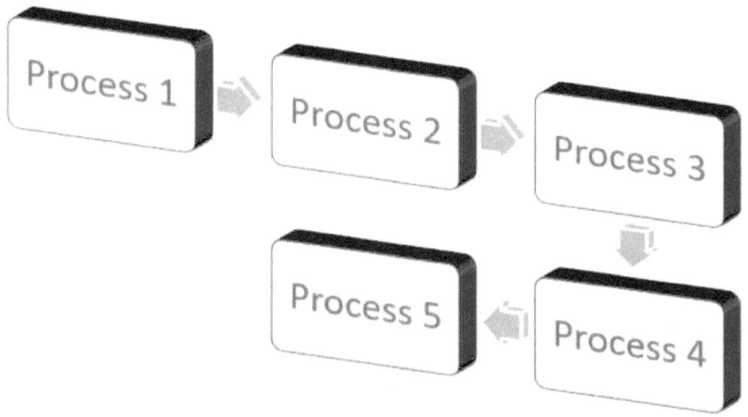

To elaborate a bit - Let's assume you are a car / bike Seller (assuming Process 3). You should know from where your agency gets the car. Let's assume it is coming from a local manufacturing plant in India (assuming Process 2) and you in turn sell it to direct consumers (assuming Process 4). In order to excel at your sale you need to understand what best Process 2 can offer and what best you can do for Process 4 - then only you can succeed at Process 3. In isolation - its success would always be limited when compared to integrated planning and focus.

NOW, once you understand to appreciate the integrated learning and focus - going against the grain needs action - Let's say you have been doing 6 steps in Process 3 - Take the challenge and see -

Why we do 6 steps - Why not 5 or why not 7 - Could there be a better way of doing it?

Once you challenge your brain with such questions - rest assured you would start seeing a change in your own performance.

If you don't improve what you do and how you do - Your career would be the same with almost the same package and entitlements!

Now deeper dive into DIRECT KNOWLEDGE – as mentioned earlier - it has two aspects

1. Functional Learning and
2. Technical Learning

Let's understand them better one after the other. We will see what do they mean and how we can facilitate that specific learning with ease.

Functional Learning

What is it?

Function can be explained as your project, business unit, department or just the team. Functional learning is to know what your team does and why.

Note: You need to know HOW you do it of WHAT has to be done and WHY it has to be done.

For example you are doing a code that helps customer to activate a new services from his mobile itself.

HOW - Get the process right: The team would have defined process that ensures everyone within team including you follow the standard coding methodology, use certain standard for defining variables or ensure some calling methods. This standardization helps to deliver good codes or product more effectively. Respect the process outlined as its developed over the years based on best practices and helps to proactively steer you clear of probable mistakes.

Respect the process – It's like an expert guide in a jungle safari – who can save your life in uncharted terrain in usual & unusual circumstances – which may otherwise be fatal.

Why does it matter?

Already have detailed it in previous section but just to reiterate and drive focus - It matters because it's a foundation of all your decision making let's see if you have to decide

- Which request is to be prioritized?
- Which requirement or work can impact Revenue?
- Which requirement or work can impact CSAT?
- Which stakeholder has to be cared for on priority?

In case you have no clue of your business / function you won't be able to put the right focus on the right things and you may end up working day and night on something trivial while something urgent and critical may take a back seat. This can have a devastating effect on your performance.

How do we go around getting better at it?

- Start with asking questions to yourself - Why are you doing whatever you are doing and how does it help the business?
- Reading the available material on your SharePoint or shared repository
- Talking to Teams which are part of your dependency chart

You have to use all the study material available to you on internal/external share points, Knowledge Database (KDB), Information repository that your project manages. One important thing or document that I always look forward to is, historical information. This historical data if captured properly helps you learn from previous mistakes and best practices. Please start using these repositories. Spend some time maybe a month and go through all the documentation available. Most of the documentation which would be relevant to you would be completed within a month and that would set you free for the rest of your life in the project because you would know the project very well. You would know your deliverables very well. You will know why something is done what was the history and why it was put in place.

Once you complete the documentation - you are already ahead of the curve and now with your regular questions you would build up a very solid foundation.

Technical Learning

What is it?

JAVA, C#, DB2,CICS,AWS,AZURE etc. These are the core technical things you must know in order to do your day to day job. You must have been hired for one of the basic technical skills and that's what our focus is in this section.

Why does it matter?

It's a no brainer why it's so important. You are hired to do something and you can accomplish that only with the required skill - now you can do it in a sloppy way that sucks or you can do the same thing with a class and quality - Your success would be completely dependent on how well you know your stuff. You need to become an expert in your domain or else you are easily replaceable.

Remember 10% experts of each industry get 90% of the earnings. Think of Actors, Doctors, Lawyers etc – Office is no different.

Think of this: When company hired you it was paying you X and you were at level Y after few years your salary has gone up to 1.5X to 2X and level is still Y. Company would easily find someone at 0.75X to do Y so with nominal training efforts *you can be kicked out.*

So ensure when your salary is increased your output must have increased as well. Hope this is simple and yet a stark truth - we all need to keep in mind!

When your salary increases by X insure your contribution, responsibility and knowledge increases by X+

How do we go around getting better at it?

Read books, white papers, apply the learning and once confident get certified. In the initial years - I would recommend try 1 certificate in a span of 9 months to 18 months in the technology. Additionally, certifications like PMP and AWS position you into global league of professionals. PMP in fact provides great opportunity to collaborate and network..

In case you follow the advice mentioned above (easier said than done) you would not have to be really worried about your technical skills going outdated because you are taking certifications & investing in learning. During the

initial 2 years spend most of your time, money and efforts in learning the basics and technology and as an outcome rest of your life in corporate would be much smoother.

Let me share an example to elaborate "why" there is a Technical Manager in Avaya in US. He is an outstanding guy. He is so thorough with so many products (that he supports) that once he is on an outage call everyone knows that issue won't last long. Whatever he says is dictum and nobody questions his plan of action and he has proven it time and again. He has stood the test of time and he has been consistently successful in recognizing the issues and providing most effective solution that's available - maestro for years! Now he has a beautiful home in US and he is a benchmark and role model for lots of people. It's not an easy achievement to attain but once attained its easy to maintain. Do you think he has to spend several hours now? No, he has spent several hours earlier in his career to set the foundation and once the foundation is set it becomes very easy to build on that foundation, year after year. He just has to learn the delta introduced by a new feature and/or technology change. With this little effort he retains his position of an expert. Once you are thorough with the basics you just have to focus on new things that have come in - let's say a new feature introduction. Whenever there is a new product release pick up the associated release document of that new product and just by going through that you would be able to understand what new has been provided because previous things are already known to you. You would have worked on it, seen it, known it and this time it's just about working out that delta.

Trick: We learn by association and if you are good with basics you easily associate and learning is easier!

Never give up, don't be afraid to ask for help when you get stuck. Learn something new every day.	Matthew Stramel

Mentorship

When only the pot is so full, the content overflows.

Only a filled pitcher can water the plant.

Only a filled cloud can quench the earth

Only a learned can mentor…..

Mentorship is a great tool to demonstrate your technical capabilities.

In today's world your individual acumen is much appreciated but not as much as of a person who has gone beyond being great himself to become a mentor or trainer. This is like stamping your capabilities and making everyone "who matters" to know that you are really able to contribute at a much higher level.

Take time to train and mentor your team and if possible other teams as well. This would help you be recognized as a brand name in your domain. More and more people would know you and at the same time you would get to know more people who may directly or indirectly contribute to your success.

I was an engineer who was a Mainframe coder but additionally served as an English Coach for TCS. Whenever I was scheduled to train people - I used to enjoy the experience and I built some lasting relationships during those trainings which helped in my career later in TCS.

Imagine that now you know things, you are training team on processes and technical stuff. You are either creating or approving the documentation for project. You have done certifications. You have knowledge about the project. You know the external and internal dependencies for you deliverable.

What do you think - how your manager would regard you?

Documentation

Documentation is a very important tool to establish yourself as a technically sound person. It's so important that we would cover this again from a different perspective. Here let's focus on some basic necessities.

Please create as many documents, knowledge base (KB) articles and White papers as you can.

Documentation helps you to become an expert because while you are creating a document you would generally do some research or at least double check your assumptions about the topic to ensure its accurate. This helps to have your signature in a document, your name is mentioned in knowledge database, SharePoint.

Whenever people refer the documentation your name repeatedly appears which reinforces your image as someone very knowledgeable. It's like writing a book - once you complete writing a book, you better be very confident and knowledgeable about your subject and once the book is published your knowledge and capability stands stamped.

That's exactly how documentation helps you in establishing your brand. It establishes you as a body of knowledge within the project. You have done so much of documentation, learnt so many things from your peers, you have crossed skilled, participated in workshops, taken certifications. This shows your strong focus on learning and it brands you as a person who is knowledgeable and is considered valuable and hence you get into the realm of the top performers. This is covered in lot more details in the later section on documentation.

Participate in Trainings

There is no better way to learn than participating in trainings. Most of the time there would be some training announced and 90% of the times you may not know about it because you are not following the notifications. At times it is dependent on manager to nominate and if manager forgets you lose an opportunity for learning new things so please make it a point that any relevant training that is happening/scheduled you should be part of it. However, you need to ensure that business is not impacted while you are going through that training. This is important because if every time your manager has to do staffing changes to support your trainings, they are not going to like it. Ensure you take care of business by extending or being available online during training or arranging a backup yourself but ensure your management do not have to intervene.

Do document what you have learnt, so that at the year-end review you would be able to tell your boss how many trainings you have attended or given and have not impacted the business because of these trainings. Your boss would most likely appreciate your efforts and you would be recognised as somebody who is knowledgeable, who is serious towards business, who is serious towards learning and also ready to help the team in the crisis that means your knowledge is not just knowledge but and applied knowledge..!

Wisdom Group or Expert Group

During any troubleshooting team refers Knowledge base of team, google/YouTube or ask seniors/colleagues. That's brilliant but you can create an additional avenue. Create a group in your organisation, maybe create a distribution list where you can ask your team members to post any technical questions even better ask other stakeholders (outside your team) to drop you a note on that particular distribution list. Take personal accountability to answer them which will ensure people find the group or distribution list useful. You can take it to WhatsApp/Facebook or any other internal Social Media available to you.

What do you get out of this? You get an opportunity to learn and your experience would be more enriched - most of the crucial learning, unfortunately, does come during issues and crisis so it's similar to learning from others mistakes/issues so you don't have to go through all the outages yourself to find the right answers - you would learn a lot and in case the same or similar situation arises in your function - you would be well prepared. This increases the sum total of your contribution. Your usefulness to the team and organization.

While working also identify avenues for learning new things. Keep an eye for competitions at intra or inter org level those challenge your core skills. You would learn a lot in the process and if you happen to win - you know you are one of the best in market and that shines in your resume as well.

"We now accept the fact that learning is a lifelong process of keeping abreast of change. And the most pressing task is to teach people how to learn."

– Peter Drucker

Chapter 2
ATTITUDE

"People may hear your words, but they feel your attitude."

— John C. Maxwell

Anybody who has spent just a few years in the organisations or corporate would be able to advise that one single thing that is valued above everything else is "ATTITUDE". Attitude is a single word which matters a lot. In case I have to put a finger on the most critical attribute that leads to success or failure I would select hands down "Attitude"

"Your Attitude determines your altitude"

Attitude is basically the way you look at things, the way you think, is basically the way your mind operates.

Attitude is a summation of several things it's not just a standalone entity and we have to be really very thoughtful about attitude.

Attitude governs your mental responses and representation of situation, responses/representation determine your action and these actions determine your outcome. Either positive or negative, your actions determine your achievements.

Even though I have rated both 'Work Ethics' and 'Positive Outlook' as 10, I would accord 'Attitude' a notch higher in weightage, and I am equating 'Attitude' with 'Positive Outlook' above.	
In my book, All other aspects are secondary and can be trained e.g. functional/technical knowledge etc but there is no training program for attitude. It's a binary - 0/1, one has it or not.	
Other aspects like discipline, integrity, time management - I consider these to be part of 'Work Ethics'	Murali Nayak

Let me quote an example - There was a point in time when Nortel was acquired by AVAYA. Leadership advised engineers and managers on both the sides to cross skill. Some people enjoyed the opportunity and happily learnt the products of both the companies and had an enriching experience while some people resisted the reality and thus the change, they continued to stick to their only line of products and you could imagine what kind of ratings, hikes and job security would have come to which set of individuals.

This sounds simple and naive but at times when we are one of them who perished, we are too reluctant to change and end up being redundant as technology and environment has gone a complete transition.

Attributes Ranking

Based on research, before we deep dive into the details it may be interesting to see what is the ranking of these attributes.

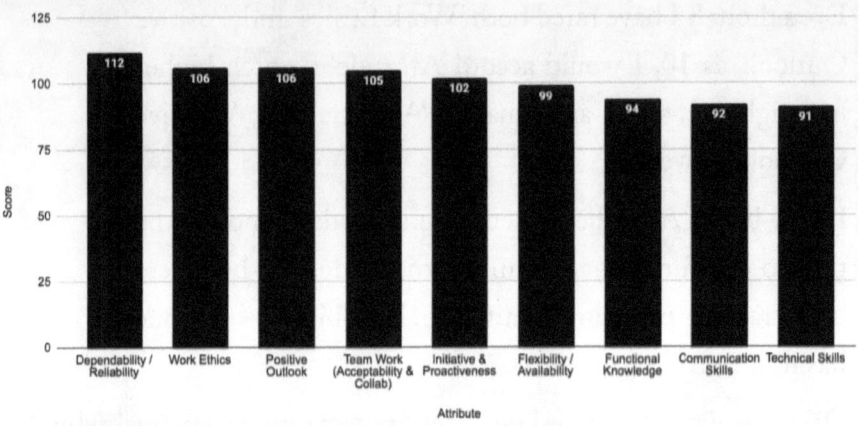

Score for each Attribute

All attributes are key to success and still there is preference from leaders for some – they suggest you shall have all of them but still what is super crucial. As per the research done with leaders here is the sequence and we will talk more about them in following pages.

Ranking	Attribute	Score
1	Dependability/Reliability	112
2	Work Ethics	106
3	Positive Outlook	106
4	Team Work (Acceptability & Collab)	105
5	Initiative & Proactiveness	102
6	Flexibility/Availability	99
7	Functional Knowledge	94
8	Communication Skills	92
9	Technical Skills	91

This is interesting to note we feel one thing is important than other but we shall see and keep in mind what matters most to the leaders. Leaders who are going to evaluate you.

Dependability and Reliability

Reliability: This appeared to be one of the most important aspect. In case you are not reliable then all your good qualities go for a toss. Imagine a *Car* that has everything, maybe the best in its class but randomly breaks down – would you be able to plan a serious long trip with it? It means you will have to be considered Reliable to be successful and such reputation has to be gradually build with consistent behaviour and efforts.

Dependable - I don't know how to stress this point enough - if you have to reach anywhere in life "anywhere", you have to be dependable. In case you are excellent technically, you are very flexible, your communication skills are outstanding, you collaborate well BUT you are hardly dependable or trustworthy for any important task. Then it's an utter waste of talent and in spite of having all the right ingredients you may not go very far.

It shouldn't happen that when some work is given to you, people still have to be worried whether it will get accomplished/completed or not. That kind of reputation is dangerous. One of the most important facets of your career is your reputation. How do we go around building the kind of reputation that helps you succeed? Reputation of someone who is dependable. It takes a lot of efforts to develop a reputation and it will not just happen with swing of a magic wand.

First step is - acknowledgement that you have to start building this credibility or reputation of dependability.

Here are few guiding principles:

1. Begin by taking work that is in your direct control and deliver it on or before time. Repeat it for at least 10 times for a variety of tasks and ensure your timely delivery is recognized or acknowledged by your required and relevant stakeholders

2. Now expand your delivery - always remember

"Under Commit, Over Deliver"

3. Once you repeat the success several times - this credibility is achieved and then your task is to preserve the same. Make it a habit to deliver anything that's committed.

Consistency

Consistency is again a very important behavioural trait. It's not like you hit the goals once and you will be successful. You have to deliver consistently before you can achieve anything considerable.

Good work is always rewarded with more work!!

Once you have performed well, people would expect more of you and you won't have a choice but to excel, again. This is not going to be easy. Now how do you check your consistency? Think from the perspective of initiatives - how many initiatives you have done so far? Are you being requested for initiatives over and over again? In case you are being requested, that means you have already established your reputation of somebody who is able to deliver one initiative after the other and with success..

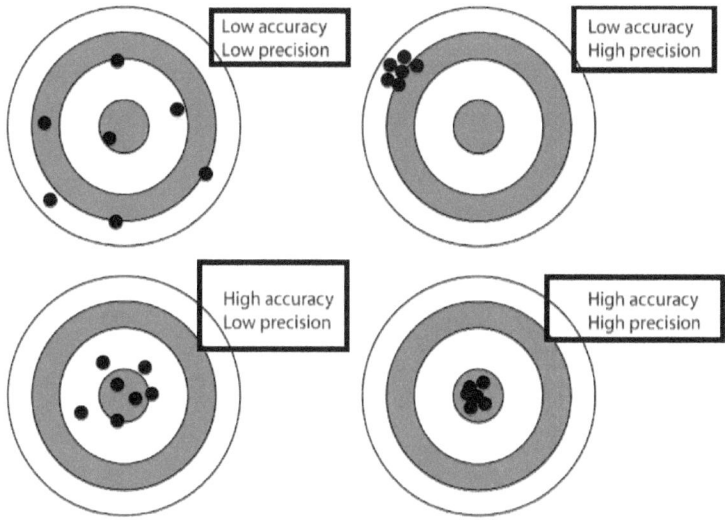

To bring home the analogy - someone who is accurate but just once is of no use but being precise is crucial. Once you are precise - moving the target to accuracy won't be as difficult. Please see the diagram below for more understanding. Someone who can shoot all arrows in the same point once just adjusts his target he would hit the bullseye every time. That consistency would mean hitting the bullseye every time and become a valuable resource for your organization. You can then demand - Hike or Promotion when suitable as you are a top performer.

Consistency of behaviour

Consistency of behaviour is paramount to prove that you have maturity and you are reliable for serious tasks. In case you are not consistent with your attitude, with your responses it becomes very difficult to trust you. Let's assume in one situation you become very polite, very humble and very dependable and at the other moment you are viewed sarcastic and filled with negativity and it's difficult to really believe in you. It gets confusing. Whether you are a nice person, a bad person or a good person or whatever.

You have to be very consistent in your behaviour, personality and results to achieve the desired level of credibility where you could be trusted with crucial and important stuff. Having said that, what you could do to become consistent?

The best shortcut is to be yourself - very simple yet so effective!

The more you try to be someone else it looks plastic so focus on being yourself. Demonstrate the real you. You should be aware of your personality, strengths & weaknesses, it gives the necessary consistency.

Make yourself comfortable with your own self. Have confidence and be prepared to take some tough decisions if required to keep yourself consistent with your identity and with your personality. Only if you are consistent with behaviour, you become a lot predictable and thus reliable.

Positive Attitude

A positive attitude helps you cope more easily with the daily affairs of life. It brings optimism into your life, and makes it easier to avoid worries and negative thinking. If you adopt it as a way of life, it would bring constructive changes into your life, and make you happier, brighter and more successful.

Positivity is something that you have to have erupting from inside out like a volcano. Everybody appreciates and loves to associate with a person who is positive some people do like to associate with people who are negative but those people are themselves negative. These people do not have much to achieve in their life and find solace in complains and lack(opposite to abundance).

Bird of feathers folk together

Pessimists associate themselves with like-minded of course negative people and they find a lot of comfort in such company. We don't have to be one of them, we don't have to be associated with negative people or be someone who spreads negativity. In case you happen to be part of a group which is very negative I would say please step away and do a favour to yourself. Keep away from them.

It's also important to know how positive you yourself are that's an interesting thing to realise.

Let's do a quick check -

Do you always look forward to going to office?

Do you enjoy talking to your colleagues?

Do you feel your manager is doing the right things?

Do you feel your organisation is doing the right things?

In case your answer was NO for any of the above question, you are somewhere treading a line of being negative. I am not saying that you are negative but you may slip to the rat hole in no time. You are close to it. Something which can happen very quickly if it is not kept in check. For example if:

You are not understanding what your manager is talking about.

You are not able to rationalize why your company is doing what they are doing.

You are not able to understand why that project has to be done in such short impossible timeline.

AND you have all the reasons why this whole request to you is baseless.

In case your manager is shouting at you or giving you feedback that you don't agree to at all.

In case you are going through any of these circumstances – my friend you need to change!!!

Now how to change from negativity to positivity? From negativity it's not an easy task, you know it's really not easy because at times you even don't know why somebody has become somebody, why you are feeling the way you are feeling. In order to start changing the perspective, the very first step would be to ACKNOWLEDGE the problem. You should try to understand that there is a problem until we realise and accept the problem it cannot be fixed.

The most important aspect here is that we cannot afford to be a pessimist.

Pessimist is like an energy sucker who wastes his energy as well as of the people around him/her.

To me technical know-how and ways and means to do a work can be learnt and varies across organizations and teams. The most important quality that makes you different is your attitude towards a problem. How do you look at a problem, how do you approach a problem, how well can you manage situations in your day to day life are some of the critical factors that I personally prefer in a team member. I strongly believe that every problem is an opportunity and it's critical and important to identify that moment and the opportunity.	Uttam Banerjee

This is really important that we get rid of any pessimist person from our group or just simply avoid that person if we cannot fire or remove that person. I would say if you are not happy and sulking – may be call in SICK spreading negativity is more dangerous & harmful than spreading pneumonia.

Positivity is non-negotiable if you are not positive you are not going to be successful!! When I say positive, it doesn't mean that you become insane and start doing or accepting anything and everything assuming that it is being positive. While you have a decent understanding of the expectations of your role develop a positive well rounded outlook. Positivity means whenever there is any decision taken by your organisation or by manager first have a positive outlook towards that, try to understand what team and org is trying to achieve and try to give your best. In case you have a difference of opinion, you shall very politely share the same with the manager or colleague specially in a one on one setting rather than going public with your thoughts.

However, it is important that if a decision is taken whether you may be in 100% alignment or not but if you are part of the team you should support by doing your bit or see if you can be excused from the project if you believe you would not be as happy. You should not become someone who opposes each and every decision because if you do that people will not really ask your opinion or they may not include you in anything significant and you may lose out opportunities to do better at your job. Being positive is not just about talking positive it's also about acting positive. Positivity is demonstrated by positive enthusiasm and positive energy. Till the time you are frustrated or you are not giving your best you are really just treading the borderline and nothing major could be achieved by sitting at the shore. You have to jump into the ring to win. A positive enthusiast is a great asset to the organisation and when I invite you to be positive I mean you have to be an enthusiastic who looks things in a positive frame of mind and supports himself and the team to achieve great heights and successful milestones. This is a common virtue of all the performers.

Attitude to collaborate

Team work & collaboration is very important	*Ajay Sharma*

Collaboration is a great precious skill and not everybody has it. Collaboration means you are able to positively work with your peers, associated teams and with your management upward & downward both side. Let me share examples of some collaborations that helped me personally. There was a situation while I was leading a Release management team and we got an escalation while working on an upgrade and the failure had come in spite of a very thorough preparation. Challenge in front of us was to scale up and ensure we do not get into the same situation again. I had a very close friend of mine who was managing another team and had certain experts for the domain. I reached out to him for help and he was kind enough to lend me some of his experts. From there we started building our own skills and grew the capabilities and in fact we made a sub team that ensured we had 100% success in upgrades. The team exists long after I left the organization and still there has been no escalation for them. It talks about the strength of the collaboration. The friendship that I had with that manager helped me to sail to shores successfully. Collaboration also doesn't always have to be work related. You can collaborate with nearby teams/business units during some official functions, get together and during the team building exercises. Once you have that kind of connect you can reach out to people outside the organisation in an unofficial setting. It pays dividends in the professional settings.

Let me quote another example of my very close friend and colleague - Amit Shukla. He made a wonderful statement once - not sure he stole or cooked it up himself but this is what he told me once

"I do professional work personally and personal work professionally"

We are still close friends and absolute fun together even outside the organisation. We used to go to the movies together, lead Rockers events together and were "no question asked" support for one another. Now, we had such a nice relationship that when there was a quality Audit for my function, he provided all the necessary documentation, support and guidance. He would have done it otherwise as well as he used to do with all other teams as it was his core expertise being QA but you can imagine the additional personal touch I had working on these Audits with him. It was a cake walk for me thanks to his pestering and insistence of arranging the required artefacts and details.

He was supportive but a bit more because he was working with his friend, helping a friend and I was also working with my friend and It helped the organisation as a whole so some unofficial settings brood some great relationships which make your job fun during official settings! Mind it he didn't make things easier for me but ensured I slog and get things right so that we are not screwed by the external auditor.

This is not just being nice but making some serious sincere deep relationships with people within the org with whom you like to spend time with. Enabling them and yourself during the hour of distress or mutually beneficial situation.

Flexibility

Flexibility is a must have in today's competitive corporate. It is important that one is flexible towards the work he does, towards the timings, towards the deliverables in summary we should be able to deliver for the business and do not get too adamant in our scope of delivery. It just cannot work in today's corporate world. Gone are the days when a person was hired for one thing and succeeded by just doing that only. The reason being, at your position itself, your colleague would be doing his work plus something more - it is a natural evolution in corporate.

How well intention setup fail when people start exploiting the company provided flexibility.

The way it has changed nowadays companies even have installed biometrics to track when a person is coming in and when the person is leaving the office. The sheer reason, people started misusing the flexibility. I myself have been very flexible to provide people work from home but I realized with more flexibility people became proportionately more demanding. It became so bad that people started putting their interest before business (at times at verge of compromising the sanity of work) and then I had to call it off. Now in this case many people who were genuinely working hard, who were really giving there every bit to the business were impacted as well. My idea was to provide this work from home facility to the folks who have been standing with business during thick and thin and this was my way to reciprocate gestures of flexibility. I learnt it from one of my manager Madhup Nagpal. Once I was in Hyderabad and planned to leave early to go for an outing with one of my colleagues, I asked Madhup if it would be okay if I left early and I offered to apply the half day, he told me that you stretch so many times so you do not need to apply this half day its fine. That was a life changing experience for me since that day I decided to award people with certain amount of leverage who demonstrated and reciprocated the same attitude. I would like to delve a bit more on this point. There was a very bright team member, his name was Ameer and I really loved working with him because he was a gem of a person, extremely flexible, knowledgeable cheerful and an amazing team player. He was always available for business and not just for me but for everybody else in the organisation. At one point of time he needed our help and it was our turn to reciprocate not just me but entire leadership rallied to help Ameer. I tried my level best to help him achieve this objective of moving to a different country, we took an exception from HR and allowed that person to work from a different country for some time so that he can figure out some solution for his existing problems. This is an example of how good work comes back to you so once you demonstrate flexibility you would realize that it comes back to you. Flexibility never goes out of fashion and another key quality of a top performer.

With COVID, things have changed a lot. Work from home has become norm. Long hours are not so uncommon but it calls a lot for personal ethics. Even for managers its tough to balance.

In companies like VMWare, Druva, CISCO etc things are much different – they are highly people centric and thus flexibility has a different dimension in their context. This also holds true for smaller start-ups. My advice here would be to evaluate the culture and adapt accordingly.

Availability

Do you work for your given number of hours? Do you reach office late and try to pack up early in the day?

To the contrary: Do you get calls from your management or your team members very frequently during your off or vacations? In case that is happening it is not good for your family life but I can tell you that you are being considered flexible by your organisation and you might get rewarded for that as well. Please see the reason people call folks on leave/out of office only when really necessary or at times they are stupid and have failed to learn anything from you. People who are stupid they have to be dealt differently and I assume your manager would not be one of them so if you are getting call from your manager at unusual hours and maybe during your vacation that shows that you are really critical and you have demonstrated a good rapport and also have positioned yourself as a very flexible individual so good job there. I'll tell you what would happen for any sensible manager such people are gems and you can literally negotiate better work, salary and promotion. It's a mutual give and take.

Important Note: The above stuff is changed completely now for the companies like VMWare, Cisco, Druva, Google etc…Where your hours are not timed but your outcomes are valued. You are not bothered over the weekend or asked to slog but some companies do insist completing the 9 hours and then a bit more so be mindful of your company and adjust accordingly. The trend is changing and management is becoming very mindful to not to bother team out of business hours but look around and adjust to culture specially focus on the outcomes and do not let them fall because of clock showed you are done for your 9 hours!

Follow ups are Frustrating!

It has been my biggest frustration that people just don't complete the work on time. At times they even never complete the task until reminded several times or are followed up with several personal nudges, emails and/or phone calls. This makes one believe that person does not care about what he has been asked to do. From your vantage point there may be a completely different perspective. You may believe that you have given all but if it's not happening it's really not a problem or not an issue at your end. I agree to it you may be the most enthusiastic person and highly committed to get this task done BUT till you keep your efforts, struggle, hard work to yourself, I don't have an update. I am blind-sided and from my perspective you are just not doing anything.

How would a person who has given a task to you would ever come to know that you have been pursuing his work so relentlessly?

So the trick is always – always – always keep your stakeholders informed

on a regular basis. It's really important that status update is available with everyone almost every day if not on hourly basis. This frequency of update should be negotiated/agreed with the stakeholders. Stakeholders should know when to expect the next outcome or an update or delivery of the required or requested product. This is very crucial in order to develop the credibility we discussed in the previous topic. This is something which I was never so careful about till one of my manager appreciated me for "Never have to follow up with you - Prashant, you keep me posted". I never realised that it is a problem with many people. I always believed, it is a right of the person to get an update from me, I wouldn't like to keep guessing if my work is being done or not. Think of your online purchases, few would disagree that their "Track Your Order" feature makes us so relaxed and predictability of delivery is just amazing.

You just can't overstate the importance of this aspect. I insisted all my team members including the managers reporting into me to ensure that nobody has to actually follow up with something that's due on our team. It has been my practice since ever and I ensure that I keep people posted on whatever I am working on. For manager managing a team it becomes even more important to ensure that your manager/reportee doesn't have to follow up with you for anything because that shows your lack of focus on the assigned task and your team would not respect you if they have to remind you over and over again about something that you are supposed to provide to them. Especially the ones reporting into you may escalate this to your manager or bring it to your attention but it should be taken up on your personal accountability to fix this. You will see the results for yourself. No sooner you implement this you would experience exponential increase in your own productivity.

Quick Test

Try to recollect how many times you have responded on something when you get a gentle reminder or may be wait till final reminder if that has happened to you in the last 6 months even twice - you are not the top most performing asset of your organisation and you have an option and an opportunity for improvement.

I personally have never been happy with anyone to whom I have to remind basic stuff and it gets on my nerves. How to improve this no follow up stuff?

> *Start with a small step and that is do not leave any email un-responded.*

Take charge

Taking charge is an important aspect that you should be working on. If you are not able to take charge you cannot grow. Opportunities would present themselves and you need to cease them. At times they come directly and at times they may come to you via hops. It would need you to be able to jump out of your comfort and known zone to grab them and demonstrate confidently your skills. You would not be able to take control of things unless you are self-reliant.

Let see an example, assume there is a problem going on in your team. There could be different responses from different people. One person would say not my job. One person would say I am not paid enough to resolve this problem. One person would say it is for the manager to resolve this and then it should be you, who could say, let me see if I can help. Now what it will do to you? It would open up number of opportunities for you at once. Firstly you are going to get your hands on something everyone else has left so that associated learning is going to be your personal trophy. You will also get brownie points with manager as you have helped him and now as you have successfully completed the task or resolved this problem you would have more confidence to tackle the next challenge. This incrementally make you build following:

1. Confidence to tackle unknown.
2. Reputation of someone who is positive and capable of sailing through uncharted waters.
3. Learning outside your team's usual knowledge average.
4. Can handle initiatives.

It's much easier to get initiatives and come into the limelight when situation appears unsurmountable and very few people are ready to take charge. In such situations, evaluate, plan, take charge and take the team successfully out of it. One important aspect is brainstorm with *all* stakeholders. Secret is someone would fix it (either you or someone else - today or tomorrow) so you have to ensure that enough light is on the issue so that it starts melting.

Your task is to just line up all whom you have access to and would be relevant to the situation.

Do not try to kill it all alone!

Do the strategic alliance or you can reach out to your manager with two to three options in your hand and ask him to let you know which one she thinks would be most suitable. Decide together and lead the execution.

Next time whenever any such situation comes up you would be the first person to be asked to lead and when a promotion opportunity comes - you may be easily positioned for the same.

If you do this your chances of getting a promotion and hike are much higher than others who are not doing it.....!!

There was a time in my job when one of my manager told in a meeting that "I want to have technical leadership in the team for Nortel products" as soon as the meeting was over I went to my desk and immediately outlined the plan about how we can go about creating that capability within the team. How the lab work would be done? How the training should be conducted? How the results be measured? With that simple email and follow through I was able to upscale my team to delivering services on this particular product in a very short span of time and my efforts were duly recognised by my manager and highly appreciated. This is just an example. There is no limit to what you can do if you choose to take charge. My idea here is to let you know and encourage you to find opportunities instead of being a bystander.

Rise up and lead - You are the top performer!!

Innovate

Innovate, learn, mentor and develop, reliable and consistent with behaviours	Anantha Amancharla

People think that it takes a genius to innovate and due to that very belief not many people really innovate. Some people have to be forced to innovate and thus organisations have to push for innovation. Org would say we need some innovation, there should be some innovative ideas coming out from each team and then all the people would wear their innovative hat and try to come out with something different or unique. There is nothing wrong with that approach but the problem is when you are forced to innovate you are not as excited as you would if you thought you wanted to innovate.

There is no limit of what you can innovate when you "want to" instead of "have to"

This is a process which is very easy and delivers millions of dollars to organisations. You might have heard of a small Indian strategy that there was a big company which was producing soap. Packing them in cardboard boxes. At times there were empty boxes delivered which hit the reputation. In order to ensure that there are no empty boxes organisation ordered a very high end X-ray machine which would scan all the boxes on the delivery line and in case it realises that it's empty it would highlight that to the floor person. Now this particular machine costed $2000 and more for upkeep. After some time there was a person from India who was having a similar problem and he just did put a small table fan that has enough power to blow away any empty cardboard box and which costed barley $10 that is the power of innovation. Very simple, unique and value propositions are outstanding.

Always engage in value innovation - there is a strategy, step by step guide on how you can innovate and there are a lot of ways in which you can innovate. It's out of scope of this book but I would recommend reading Edward De Bono for getting some brilliant ideas on how to innovate and think out of the box. Once you deliver a significant value to your business your business would remember you for years. Innovation could be a product, innovation could be a process. Innovation could be anything but baseline is there has to be innovation and YOU have to do it. The time, money, effort or head count you save for your org contributes towards your success and your objective of being the top performer.

Integrity/Work Ethics

A single lie destroys a whole reputation of integrity.

– Baltasar Gracian

You may be successful in the short term but it's unimaginable to do extremely well in your career with questionable ethics. I have worked with great leaders and in great numbers. One thing which is common with all of them is - they all are very high on integrity.

If you have integrity you are respected, if you have integrity people know that you would tell black as black and white as white they don't have to judge you or cross question your statements or look at you with suspicion.

It's always the truth that wins sooner or later and prevails. There has been a situation with one of my friends where there was integrity issue with the manager himself. He was asked to hire someone and he was promised to get a share in the joining bonus thankfully my friend didn't participate in this and the person who was hired was not suitable for the position. However the referral money was distributed and it was unknowingly given to my friend as well. My friend returned the amount very next day. Years after this instance there was an investigation and people who were involved in unethical practices were asked to leave. All of a sudden they found themselves struggling along with their families because they had no job the very next day. Companies are never soft on people who have integrity issues so it's not optional, it's non-negotiable. It's the most important value that you have to demonstrate if you have to be successful and that's integrity because sooner or later you would be outsmarted.

Work Ethics is most important and comprise of lot many things. People should have high Work Ethics	Krishna Pandey

Just to bring this home. There was a serious situation in an organization where one of the manager instructed three of his reports to claim illegitimate hotel bills and he used to approve them. These folks were supposed to pay him the money once reimbursed by the org and these folks were given a part by marking them in night shift roster (while they were actually not there in the shift) and paid hefty night shift allowances. One day this craft came to the management attention - the manager was fired and other folks were also taken for a task and gradually all of them were rated low and driven outside the organisation. With these examples I am trying to say sooner or later these things come to surface then perpetrators feel humiliated and lose all the respect they may have earned. The problem is - our industries are fairly small places and nobody forgets such things.

Rest assured, you will not be hired by anyone in case you happen to be party to any such stuff. In case anyone is requested for feedback about you or during background verification and if you are involved in any such thing you will not get favourable feedback and then you might not get a job when you need it the most. This is my warning a very strict warning to not to indulge in any misadventure of this sort. Pursue integrity sepite all odds. Do not bend in for this integrity even if your management, senior management or even HR asks for it. Find someone who is incorruptible. In case you feel right till CEO all are involved and want you to do something that's not ethically right - You would be better in a different company than this one. Long term achievers/Top performers are very high on integrity.

If you do not have integrity you won't have a great career!

| Hardworking and integrity | Wasi Abidi |

Amicable yet assertive

Assertiveness in broad terms is a part of communication skills and holds its own value. In case you are not assertive enough you will not go very long. Why is that so? Assertiveness is not something that comes to everyone naturally but it's mandatory once you rise up the ladder. In case there is a need to learn assertiveness you better take a course for the same. Assertiveness prevents you from being pushed around. Defends you from unacceptable submissions.

The best and the straightforward method to be assertive is to talk with facts. Data speaks louder than thousands of statements. Prepare and present data, you would start seeing your assertiveness take a leap. Please practice this if you are not doing it already and if you identify this gap, trust me it has to be fixed as quickly as you can.

Team work

Teamwork is the most commonly spoken word. Every other team member would say let's do a team work. Now what is teamwork? Teamwork calls for collaboration and until you are really good at collaboration you will not be able to achieve the outcomes that you have been hired for. Even if you have been in the team for a while and you cannot collaborate it's very difficult to achieve the objective of the team in general. All the successful managers I have been opportune to work with have been excellent collaborators. I haven't seen a person who cannot gel well with teams or individuals and still make a great success story.

Teamwork doesn't begin when your finger is pointed out, it begins when the finger is pointed inwards. It is like a savings account. You would have to submit something into the teamwork account and then only you would be able to retrieve it. Before even you think somebody should help you, think if you have helped the other person earlier? In case you have not helped the other person then you shouldn't be expecting him or her to help you because they have no obligation to help you. You have to start helping others so that when you need a return favour it's easier as the other person (at least to some extent) feel he has to do this to return a favour that he enjoyed some point in the past.

"Return of the favour" is easier to get than a "favour"!!

In the first you owe something from others while in later you are at the mercy of good will, mood, situation etc - Which may not line up always.

This is a very important lesson now how do you start if you have been a sucker in teamwork?

It's a very small saying get down to office tomorrow first of all say good morning to everyone or good afternoon if you are in the afternoon shift so it make them feel comfortable that you are a human being and know how to say hi & hello. I am sure mostly this may not be necessary but this is mentioned for folks who are completely recluse.

Now, once you have given them first shock that you are saying hi, or good morning to them be prepared to give another shocker. Try to spend some time with them and see if there is something that they are struggling with where you can be helpful for example when I used to go around after completing my work I used to ensure that I understand what each team member is working on. What is it technically and how does it fit in the larger scheme of things. I was very good in excel sheets and if somebody was struggling with data I would sit with them for hours maybe but ensure that their life is comfortable after that. Similarly in case I found somebody was struggling with work and they will not be able to complete within the shift and I had some time I used to share that work without any expectations. You know what, next time whenever they found an opportunity to help me they were also eagerly helping me and there was never an issue of not getting enough support for myself. I have enjoyed it so much that I naturally look forward to it.

Being President of the engagement committee gave me an opportunity to work with some of the finest people in the organisation. These folks were always charged up and have an overflowing contagious enthusiasm. I was opportune to have company of core team - especially Noorain, Seema, Rupali Sundar and Juhi Gorwara - So many people with same mindset to make things happen - contagious energies and phenomenal teamwork!! It was so much fun that I spent 2 to 3 hours beyond my shift to ensure that we are running great events across the country. I can't explain the adrenaline level that used to pump up while working on these events. It was just fantastic. I am sure there would have been enormous dopamine as well that used to give such a great feeling that's beyond words. Now imagine if I was not a great team player I would have not been included in this group and I would have missed most of these memorable moments of my work life which I cherish. Teamwork is non-negotiable if you want to speed up your growth and career.

Top Performers are Team performers as well.

Walking the extra mile

This is an interesting topic - going the extra mile, what does it mean? It means that you would not limit yourself to the things that you have been asked to work on. Work for salary - 8 to 9 hours and you would be earning bread and butter. Once you invest beyond your shift hours in learning, in understanding, in helping team in project / initiatives, in extracurricular activities, in capability development, that is your fuel for faster growth. There is no end to how much you can achieve by just spending additional 1 or 1.5 hour with right intentions. I do not suggest slogging for 10 to 12 hours because you waste day in cafeteria, chatting with colleagues on useless stuff, greasing your managers ego etc.

You don't have to invest this additional time with the people who do not come to the office to work or getting better at their career. They are the people who just come to kill time and go back home and do minimal to keep the jobs.

So first of all you have to be highly productive and not engaging in the stuff that takes away your crucial time of office work.

First and foremost, you have to complete your basic office work then only you can/shall think of any initiative or anything else!!

All initiatives are useless if your primary work is in jeopardy!

First and foremost thing for any success at job is - you should know how to be good if not best at what you are hired for. You should be able to deliver all the work that is expected from you and that too with high quality. If you suck in your basic delivery/deliverables nobody cares how good you are in other initiatives.

I learnt this hard way because while I started my job in TCS I was a stupid jerk. I was barely interested in doing mainframes development but I was always interested in doing initiatives so I was running more initiative than my whole team put together. One fine day I kept a presentation for my management team to show them a novel idea - I had planned an initiative to gather ideas from global team and to my surprise my management was not impressed and instead he gave me an hour long lecture. He said you are not hired here for initiatives - you are here for mainframe development and you better get yourself working on the codes and deliver the applications.

I was too new at that point of time in my career to understand why the manager was talking like that and I really hated him for it. It was long after I became a manager, I realised what my previous manager meant when he said - deliver your work first and initiatives later.

It was an eye opener for me. The most basic thing that you have to do is, do your job. Only when you are thorough with your job, you should spend time, energy and work on initiatives. Then only it will be appreciated. You may think, you will do a clumsy job on your day to day deliverables and be an outstanding resource because you are doing lot number of initiatives, it's not going to work.

Initiatives are absolutely necessary as they provide you opportunities to expand your perspective, to mingle and interact with folks from other walks of life and line of business. For example I learnt excel sheets not during my work but during initiatives.

Going Extra mile is absolutely necessary but only after going through the mandatory miles.

Select Your Initiatives wisely

Not all the initiatives are worth your time. Try to engage in initiatives after careful evaluation.

Few aspects to select from available initiatives are:

- Revenue impact.
- Hierarchy Levels to which this would benefit. Like
  - Level 1 - Your Manager or
  - Level 2 - Your Manager and His Manager or
  - Level 3 - Your Manager, His Manager and His Manager and so on
- Teams Impacted or benefitted.
- Technologies Involved.
- Complexity - the More the merrier.
- Future relevance.

There could be a lot more aspects but these basics would help you to make an informed decision.

Develop your brand

Identity and reputation management is very important and it has to be carefully crafted. It won't be made in one day. It's a tiring effort and has to be done with consistency. You just cannot be successful until your reputation is of someone who is really good and reliable.

Think of it like the brand you trust in when you look at cars. You look at Audi and BMW differently while at Toyota, Datsun and Maruti differently. Trust me, all these car manufacturers give their best to ensure they deliver the highest level of quality, fuel efficiency, design to perfection they are capable of but you do not consider them equal to premium brands and they are definitely tagged at a very different price tag. Audi and BMW are dream cars for some people while for average Indian Maruti and Datsun may not be a dream car anymore. The brand once developed easily commands premium and is paid for. Please note, I am not commenting the Advanced technologies / features these cars are laden with - reference comparison is to just drive home a comparison of branding. Like for Maruti - they wanted to roll out Kizashi - an ultra-premium car and it failed as customers couldn't relate. That's one more reason Maruti rolled out there another version NEXA with an upmarket feel and services.

Similarly, you need to make your brand. Once brand is ready you can charge a premium and this doesn't happen overnight. It takes a lot of hard work, commitment, innovation, sophistication, out of the box thinking to achieve this but once you have achieved rewards, recognition and returns come in avalanches.

Now the question is how do you go around building this brand for yourself? Here comes the power of marketing.

In Hindi there is a saying

"Jo Dikhta Hai Woh bikta Hai"

that translates into whatever is seen is sold so you might be doing hundreds of great things but until unless there's somebody to recognise that and appreciate it - it's of no use at least for you.

You have to ensure that whatever good you are doing is published appropriately and have to start doing it right from tomorrow once you reach your office!!

Top performer's work talks for them
but ensure its loud enough!

I will give you another example - there was a certificate issue that could have infected all the customers of my company and might have caused some downtime to each one of them. My colleague led this project and she completed it successfully but when there was a time to really tell the success story she presented it very politely suggested

"my team has completed certificate install for so many customers"

then I advised her instead of saying what you just said the same thing should be presented from revenue or business impact standpoint. And this is what I said

"There was a serious situation where all of a sudden more than 300 customers would have found themselves out of business for at least 24 hours impacting their revenues for at least a few millions and our company would have also got penalties slapped for so much of downtime. I would like to thank the team that worked overnight and over the weekend to effectively address this problem. I was surprised with the excellent execution by team and I would request leadership to help me reward and recognize my team appropriately for their hard work and customer value they delivered"

Now think of it, my colleague was absolutely right in her approach of telling just the basics and that's what most of us do. Now a person of a stature of my colleague who is already highly respected and regarded in leadership may not need this individual instance to market herself or her team but for individuals who are still learning and are at the start of their career, maybe in the new company or in the existing one you need to understand how to market and position your accomplishments. Note: I am not encouraging falsehood but ensuring all associated accomplishments are highlighted - value is presented. I just put the actuals on table which were missing earlier in the plain vanilla statement.

There was a fantastic and very respected colleague in CISCO he was an outstanding technical resource. When he talks you can hear him for hours and he can explain to you the most complex Cisco related Complex technical stuff with absolute ease. While he was technically great rather brilliant he also had a knack of positioning himself appropriately. He never made an agenda to tell about his achievements but he would ensure that during the conversation you would have realised what great stuff he has done for you, for the organisation, for the customer and the management. I would repeat without making it sound like one.

So for example, he won't tell you that he is an excellent technical resource on video devices he would rather tell you a story when there was some big issue and how he steered the whole team and customer out of that problem. You would realise that this guy is really outstanding when it comes to video solutions and he truly deserved every bit of it. Let me quote an example here.

One day, he got a call from super boss Ajay Sharma to help a Sales engineer who was at customer site in Sri Lanka and having issues with some endpoints during customer visits. I was sitting in front of him the day this conversation took place. Then in the next 30 minutes or so he helped the guy in Sri Lanka and things were sorted"

Now, since then within a span of 6 months I heard him at least 3 times sharing this story at various opportunities, smoke breaks - it was unintentional - he was not even doing it for the sake of recognition but with this repeated iteration of this fact - how helpful he was during a crisis - surely builds his rapport and presents him from a position of strength. This is an example where you shall be prompt to present your good work on suitable occasions with care not been tagged as a bragger!

This is just how you have to ensure that you do not have to always tell very clearly that "Ok! I have done this, I have done that" because if you do that after sometime people do not value it and they will say this person is always boasting about himself so you have to learn to be famous, to be able to market yourself but without being so obvious!

Try this out - make a list of what you have done that needs and qualifies for recognition. Once you have done that, find an appropriate occasion to publish and present it. For example if you have done an initiative and only you know about it and the team that has participated - it's high time that you figure out who all need to know about it and who will matter. Let's say, you think your senior leadership should be aware of it - create a PPT slide. May be two or three slides to summarise the achievements and then design few certificates and get them self-signed, by immediate manager and the leader whose opinion matters or to whom this publicity needs to reach.

There is another effective way to proactively market something if you are working on a project or an initiative, try to bring it in meetings, coffee talks, lunch tables or wherever appropriate with the appropriate audience. If you can create mailers which are attractive that would be a great added advantage. You should always try that any work you do receives an appropriate amount of publicity and attention.

"Greatest of work in Corporate if not showcased demotivates the team and people who have put the hard work!!"

Chapter 3

COMMUNICATION SKILLS

Have you met people who are technically excellent but not doing great in their careers just because they struggle with their communication skills? It's not unusual to spot people in corporate that haven't made large or failed to some extent due to their communication skills.

Right from your college when you first think of campus selection or career - people tell you - focus on your communication and language skills followed by interview, group discussion and presentations. I believe it's so TRUE - during campus we have seen, people with better presentation and communication skills are selected ahead of the folks who lack fluency or do not hold strong command over language.

While talking about communication skills following aspects should be your focus areas.

Verbal

This is the most basic aspect of communications. Selection of words also plays a very important role so you need to focus on your vocabulary. After evaluation of several books I can say Word Power Made Easy happens to be the most effective book on the topic so if you have not gone through it already please pick it up and finish it. This is a must have!!

It will introduce you to new words and that will help you put forward your point more effectively and positively.

I repeat - Complete the Word power Made Easy
by Norman Lewis.

Another important aspect is to ensure when you talk - you talk based on the learning style of the audience/person.

Different people learn differently. There are three basic learning preferences:

Learn them as you need to adjust your tonality accordingly to be more effective with respective people.

Visual

People who are visual learners they want to look at everything or imagine everything vividly as a picture before they can learn. Such people usually talk at a very fast pace. They have a lot of details popping up in their mind which they would like to share with you. You'll find them talking very quickly and at times even skipping a word or two. For these people you need to speak in a decent pace otherwise they would lose interest and you would loose their attention.

Auditory

These people are slow with their pace of talking and just in case you go ahead and tell them a lot of stuff at a speed of any visual person they might miss a lot of details, so you need to be very careful.

Now the question is - how do you identify them? You can identify these people by paying attention to the selection of words while they talk. Look at people using generic words like "I can hear that" or they may say "it sounded like…", "that sounds great" while someone who is more visual would say something similar to "it looks great" so please pay attention while you're talking to someone. Plan to cater to both types of audience.

Kinesthetics

These people are generally the ones who feel things/emotions. Everything that is presented has to make an emotional connect to pervade through them. They need to create an emotional connect before they can really appreciate what they are being told. So they need even more time than auditory learners you can spot them by the selection of their words and speed of speech. They say "it feels right" or something like "it felt nice" etc. so you need to slow down further. Let them have their time of absorption.

**In case you are to address a large Audience - ensure you are making space for all the 3 types of learners. That is why Videos have more appeal as they touch all the three aspects - Audio, Video and Kinesthetics.

Non Verbal

70% of all our communication happens through body language so you can understand the importance of getting that right and you just can't afford to go wrong here. You have to take care of this to ensure you are not losing on 70% of your communication.

You should focus on your body language in case you are going to talk in person. Your body language is extremely critical which also includes the way you dress up, the way you show up. In case you are wearing a loose jeans and t-shirt, hip-hop cap you will not gain the confidence of an audience which is looking up for someone serious and who can deliver. I don't deny that you would have capability but still the perception plays a lot bigger role than you can imagine. I know it's changing now. Especially in start-ups you can expect leaders in jeans (considered to be an informal wear) and addressing the audience and I won't dictate you once you are at that level of success but till the time you aren't there, please take care of your clothing.

I would not currently take you through a lot of details of body language that's one of my favourite topics but few things I would really like to highlight:

Open Hand Gestures

There is something which has been in fashion for ages and history goes back to the point when people used to live in jungles where open hand gesture generally indicate that you are honest, not holding anything that may pose a danger to the other person. Open palm/hand suggests that you are telling the truth at least the truth that you are aware of or believe in. It suggests that you are not cooking up while talking. Do not kill yourself for doing that. In case it is hampering your performance you can ignore but by all means folding your hands for a major part of your presentation would not send across a very positive message about the content that you have delivered. Please be very careful about your hands in case you are used to crossing them.

Eye Contact

It happens to be another critical parameter in the communication. I know by this time you all are grown enough to understand that a confident talk is always followed up with deep piercing eyes which reinforce the fact that you are talking about what you believe in. In case there are more than one person you are trying to address, please ensure that there is a proper eye contact with everyone. Do not miss anyone in the room because you never know who is the decision maker and who is the influencer and I am sure you would not like to get wrong with them. Again this all shouldn't freak you out but you should be mindful of this!

Fidgeting

Fidgeting is an interesting phenomenon where the anxious energy tries to channelize itself by varied involuntary actions - Which includes tapping your fingers, too much shaking, wobbling voice, too much motion around the available space, going forward and backward unnecessarily - in summary we need to control this. Now question is "How"? Answer is only one "Practice your content". Know it by heart and practice it in front of a mirror while you prepare for the big day. Please do not take it for granted.

Please note this is not uncommon to have some motions, hand movements, minor to and fro movement around podium that is acceptable unless your movements start interfering your quality of delivery.

Posture

Generally speaking of person with confident body language would tend to stand tall. There is a relationship between our state of mind and body language that is why while you are standing straight upright, looking at horizontal level or maybe slightly above the horizontal level in combination with shoulders pulled back - that gives you a different confidence level and based on the posture your brain gets a signal that you are confident and be able to tackle things with ease. This also emanates from a historical, primitive posture of fighting - We all are animals by biology and we still respond accordingly, so if you look at animals while they are about to fight or mate they would project themselves as large as possible. That is how the brain operates. So, keeping it simple - whenever you are getting into your presentation next time please ensure that you are standing tall, confident, looking into the eyes of your audience and do not forget to top it up with a nice smile - a genuine one. I repeat a genuine one. The made up smile which is just from the lips doesn't help.

"Smile from your eyes":)

Power of Dressing

Whenever you are dressing up please ensure some basics which I am sure you would already know but I feel it's my responsibility to reiterate that dress with your best clothes and carry yourself apt for the occasion. Corporate is changing now and people are becoming more acceptable towards informal wear in corporate rooms but still try to keep it as professional as you could.

Power dressing helps individual to present their position and authority in business/workplace.

"Dress for the position you aspire for"

Power dressing has a major impact on your career. I learnt this through a book long ago and since then I always ensured that I am aptly dressed - at times it's okay to be overdressed for the occasion and almost always better than underdressed for the occasion or situation. I will not be explaining here what you should wear in a given situation. You can check out YouTube and internet for various options and you would find some good explanations.

PPT - PowerPoint Skills

Corporate stories are mostly told on Slides. Your story better be loud and crisp!

Let me admit there is no single way about how PPT should be made but still there are few guidelines that may help.

5 × 5 Rule

Your slide should not have more than 5 lines and 5 words per line because if you put a lot of material in a slide, your audience end up reading the content while you try to sell or speak your points. Focus should be to ensure all required content is there and it is succinctly presented.

Dumb Numbers

All the numbers should line up which essentially means anybody should not be able to find mistakes in the numbers. For example, in one portion of PPT you will suggest 10 as a quantity and then further drill down or that 10 lines up only to 8 or may shoot up to 11 or more - that won't be great and you would end up losing the plot and maybe considered - careless.

Sample Items	Quantity
Books	10
Pen	15

Books Category	Quantity
Fiction	5
Self Help	2
Technical	2

Here if you see Books Category Table if counted would show (5+2+2 = 9) while first table shows 10 books. This is CRIMINAL. Please never ever do that and cross check all the numbers in your ppt

"Some people in meeting have Fault Finding as their full time job!!"

Backup Slides

You cannot dump everything on your main slide as it may get too overwhelming and may not be relevant either. However, you need to ensure that any relevant data which might be needed, should be available in the backup slides but not in your main one. This has to be planned very carefully. Try to use hyperlink option of Microsoft ppt and it would give an additional professional look. I generally have a blank slide named as "Backup Slide" that's just after the THANKS Slide and post that you can have all your back-up slides.

Pre guess Questions

You shall review your content yourself and if someone can do a double check that's always helpful. Try to get as many questions as you can based on that content you plan to present. It would make you more prepared for the occasion and you would have proactively arranged all the required artefacts, just in case required.

Review the trend

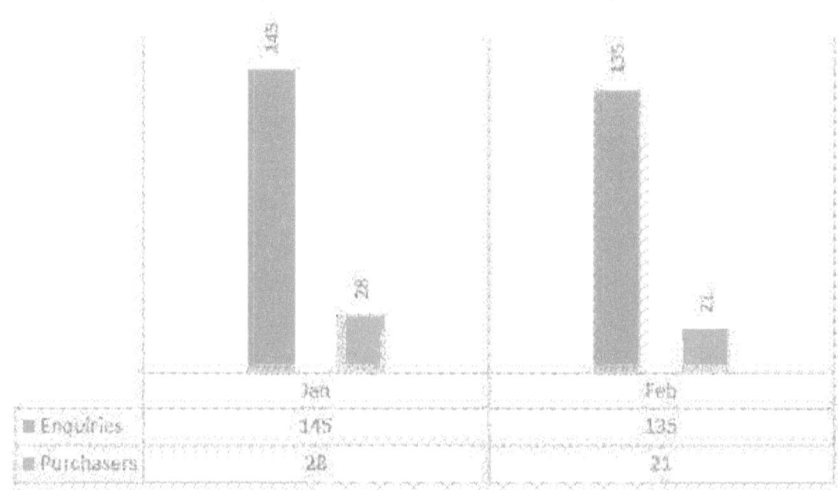

Review the data and wherever you find any deviation - get that answered logically to yourself. Arrange reason for such deviations. Observe the graph below - Do you see any deviation or potential question if you were presenting it?

Answer: Graph at its view looks fine and a simple but observe following. That while Enquiries are just less by 7% drop in purchasers is as high as 25 %!! This is easily missed unless properly observed.

	Jan	Feb	Difference	Percentage Change
Enquiries	145	135	10	7 %
Purchaser	28	21	7	25 %

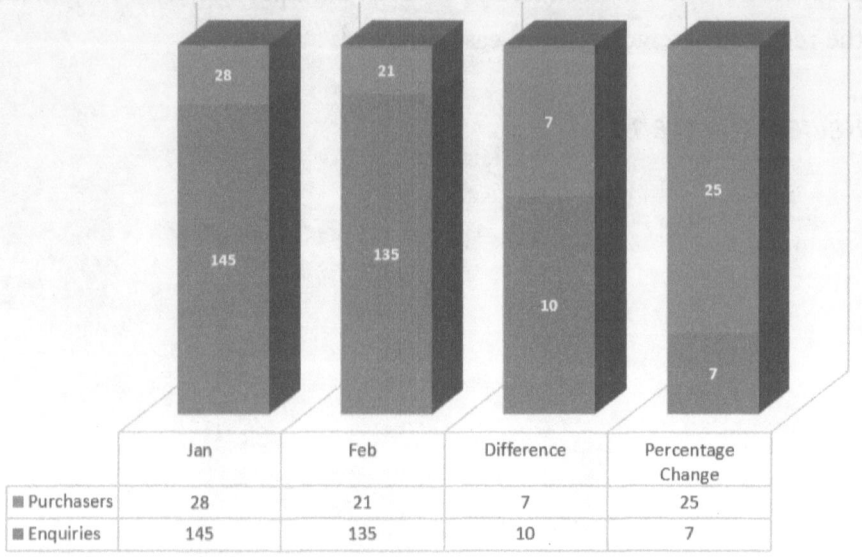

Have Stories and Excitement

Since childhood we are told stories and human beings are good at remembering stories - We need to leverage that natural advantage as people give more attention to stories than the numbers. Lot of numbers with no story is not exciting but having a story with a lot of Numbers or even less numbers would do well when it comes to presentation. Have your stories ready before your presentation.

There should be a tangible amount of excitement in yourself so that the person in front also appreciates and understands the greatness of what you are talking about.

A quick story here – Once at one of my old firm, we did an outstanding employee event and post the event the Participating Engineers called the organizing team for a surprise Pizza Party - We all were so overwhelmed. Now, while we were presenting this success story to Leadership, they appreciated the numbers but this story of Pizza party went a long way. We received appreciation for work in many forums and always a special mention of this party. The reason it stayed in everyone's mind? Obviously, the gesture itself was significant and at the same time it made our story complete.

"Know your audience"

Know what your audience would be motivated/ excited to hear: Nobody comes to listen to what you have to say. What matters is - what they want to listen or what are they looking forward to? In case, there are several stakeholders, please be mindful of who might have interest in what topic. Do not ignore any stakeholders during the presentation; plan your presentation well ahead of time. Do this

Create a quick list of diverse stakeholders.

Create a list of interest of these stakeholders.

Consider how are you addressing them.

Is there any exciting news/information for each of them?

This list would help you to ensure that no major stakeholder is left unattended and unaddressed.

Time Management:

It is absolutely necessary that you spend a decent amount of time in planning your time. There is no point in spending all the time you have got on first few slides and leaving no time for some important aspects that may be covered in the later slides. Plan for just 85% of your time and leave 15% of your time for any exigency or questions which may come through during the presentation. In case, you have packed your deck for complete 100% time - you are very likely to end up missing covering some of the aspects due to lack of time.

Preparation and Demo practice

No Presentation, I repeat - No presentation should be given unless you yourself have gone through slides at least twice and you are sure what you are talking at each slide. This is very important - we always know what we want to speak on a given slide but you would be amazed to see how much value add happens when you repeat the presentation by yourself.

Emails

Emails are your day to day mode of communication and a lot you do or get done is over emails so you better be good at it. Few aspects of email that have to be there whatsoever.

- Not many people read line by line of long winding email so please put the information that is absolutely necessary.
- Do structure your response and just don't throw away information all over the place with no structure.
- For large emails, ensure you do have a Summary or Overview at the beginning so that people don't have to find a needle in a haystack. Let detail section be there for whoever wants to delve into it.
- Use tables instead of long statements - they represent information in a better way.
- Setup a Rule for outgoing emails – "1" Minute delay or more to avoid any unwarranted email going out or missing out on attachment. It protects you against those oops moment. Refer Appendix 2 for link on how to do it.

Chapter 4

DOCUMENTATION

Documentation is something that would never go out of fashion.

People work/decide & act on perceptions –
Perceptions are based on what people interpret.

Documentation is an extremely necessary habit and mostly taken for granted. We leave a lot to our memory and then struggle when it's required the most.

It's advisable to document each and everything that's important, otherwise we may end up being people dependent.

Imagine a situation where a person in your team does lot of critical work and hasn't shared anything with anyone - what would happen - if the person leaves the organization? Complete Team and Organization can get impacted or everything would need to be done from scratch.

In order to avoid such hazards, documentation shall be done preferably daily or at least once a week. Managers shall ensure that they are not leaving this important piece at the discretion of the team but is evaluated at his level.

What kind of documentation and why we shall stress about it?

Daily Work

Day to day - a lot of work gets done. You create/modify or remove an asset or may do some operational work. However if it's not quantified or documented - it would be difficult to recall so much when you sit for your performance review and also even if you want to get some details on your own work.

Please maintain a simple excel sheet and start using it TODAY.

Sample of most simple Tabular format:

Date	Task
01 Jan 20xx	Completed Code for Alpha Beta Project
02 Jan 20xx	Completed QC for Micro Mist project

This would help you to easily recall and make meaningful presentations for any reviews.

If you are a manager then this is more critical because you might have your team members who may come back to you with their logs of work and you may not have any reference to validate whether they are accurate or not. In spite of their good intentions at times people tend to mistake and if you do not have such notes, logs and reference for yourself, you may have no choice but to trust your team member.

Sample provided below for reference

Date	Task	Completed By	Escalation/Kudo/Neutral
25-Apr	Outage was managed so well on XYZ customer system	Sam Thompson	Kudo
27-Apr	Wrong Files were shared with Customer	Tarzo Phil	Escalation

Your Created Asset

In case you happen to create some kind of code or sop or any other product. There has to be a great user manual. In case you don't do it, your project or product is yet incomplete. There is always an inclination to showcase the world what you have produced – which is a great psyche and anybody would love to do it but you should go slow and ensure you deliver a complete package. You have provided all the guidance and information that a person might ever need while using your product, it demands a special focus at your end to provide all the relevant documentation. Do not forget to save it in a common repository where it is accessible to everyone.

Performance discussion action items

This is an interesting one. How many times you have your appraisal discussion with your manager without ever documenting anything and then you are surprised during one on ones - in spite of all your hard work why are you not being given the best available rating? The reason is you and your manager never agreed to the common objectives. You might have done your best and you may have also achieved what you felt your manager wanted from you but its insufficient.

"Your good may not be Manager's good enough!"

So the trick is to document the agreed performance indicators or expectations in a measurable/doable/quantifiable action items.

"You need to do great customer service" → *Can't be achieved as you don't have a reference.*

"You have to ensure CSAT is >98%" → *This can be achieved as its quantifiable and measurable. Disputes are reduced as you and your manager are talking about same reference.*

My wife had a colleague who was a consistent top performer. During one of their conversations, she mentioned to my wife that I have completed all the tasks agreed with manager during my performance review. I was surprised why such a small thing never crossed my mind. We had just started our careers so this came to us as a delight and there onwards I started using it. I completely saw the merit in this process. The logic is simple, while you are sitting across the table with your manager and you document each feedback and associated action item then you start working and start closing each of these action items. This would help you to quantify the outcome. By end of agreed time, either you would have achieved all what your manager has asked you to do or you would have provided a reason if there was a failure. This documentation would help you to prove to your manager that whatever feedback was given and whatever expectations were set at the beginning are met and now your manager won't have a choice but to agree that you have achieved whatever targets were given to you. Your manager may not heartily appreciate this every time as you are kind of legalizing things;)

However, be very careful not to take targets which may be too difficult or completely out of scope. Do negotiate with your boss and set realistic goals which are challenging and fun to achieve while they contribute towards your learning.

Team/Project work

In case your team has worked on a project there must be a technical documentation as we discussed above but there has to be a marketing material created by you. This particular material would be significant and critical to ensure the success of your project is not just published within your business but has far reaching appreciation and returns.

You have to invest at least 10 to 15% of the time that you spent on project to create great documentation. Your performance on your project would completely be determined by the perception of people and management about the project so it's important that you really have a great face to show. Your project has to be packaged in absolutely brilliant saleable format. Do ensure that you have the following things created for your project.

- PPT that summarises the business outcome, the team, the methodology, reusability, the journey. It would be your spokesperson.
- Email - A catchy email that can summarize and communicate the great work done.
- A Poster - ensure some hard copies of such posters are pasted on notice boards - which would help position your project across floors. Might have limited feasibility please plan accordingly.
- Leadership Snippet Mail - Based on your leadership's preference find a ladder/means to ensure senior leadership is also aware of what you have done & accomplished.

"Even before you spend a moment on any project - ensure it is aligned to objectives/priorities/pain areas of your management and leadership. This has to be the MOST important parameter of deciding a project!! Period..!!"

MOM (Minutes of Meeting)

This is like a dessert after a delicious meal. No Meeting shall end without a proper Minutes of meeting and action owner assigned to it. Unless you do that - you are just wasting time of all as no work gets done. There is no accountability, hence, no result.

You shall ensure the following things are captured and shared with everyone involved.

- Participants in the meeting.
- Highlights.
- Important Decisions Taken.
- Action Items.
  - Who is responsible.
  - Who is Accountable.
  - Expected Time of completion.

These are minimal things to be included in the MOM.

In the next meeting, on the same topic when you would carry this MOM - it shows your professionalism and also gives confidence to other participants that the work is being done and actions being tracked.

Chapter 5

UPWARD MANAGEMENT

If any time in the past you felt that your manager was not important then let me tell you friend, that you have been wrong all those times. You would understand that in a while.

Why is it so important to focus on upward Management?

Be excellent at your role, beyond that find out the priorities of your manager and help support those	Anurag Bahadur

First let's talk about upward management: How do you manage your leadership, your managers, your peers who are senior to you - why this is so important? It is vital because they are your customers. You, as a product are as valuable as perceived by your management and they happen to be your public interface. Unless you have a great relationship with your manager and leaders it may be increasingly difficult to attain any great success in your career and so we need to focus on how to ensure that your upper management is fine or happy with your work? They have access to forums where you are not present but to grow, your name shall be in those forums - that can only be achieved when you get this thing right!

Timely Reverts and update

If I have to highlight a single important thing, I would probably bet on this particular aspect. As a manager you always need work to be done in a timely manner because some next level person might have asked for that. It becomes extremely important that it is delivered within the stipulated time. In case you are anticipating any delays- do shout it out so that your manager can do anything that may be necessary to mitigate the delay. This shouldn't be a SURPRISE EVER!!

There should never be a need for follow-ups because follow-ups are wastage of energy of management and if manager has to chase you for something a few times it would be better to do it themselves. Most of the managers are definitely capable of doing what they have asked you to do. This also shows we are not so careful or prudent about their requests and taking it for granted or lack sincerity - *while we may be treating it with the highest priority.*

Whenever any task is given to you please ensure that it is delivered well in time. If there is any challenge that you expect, please give them a call/ heads up. Discuss the alternative so that they do not end up in surprise at the time of delivery. Once I did a big mistake of not informing my project lead that I was not able to develop the code at the speed I should have been because I was struggling technically. At the last moment when delivery was due next day I informed my manager that I am sorry but I will not be able to deliver it tomorrow. I am nowhere close to completing the code. He was obviously not impressed and unfortunately he didn't have time to show his anger or anguish. We immediately jumped onto writing the code. He and I sat through the night and completed the code. He was an expert and thus completed the code in time. It saved the day thanks to the leadership he demonstrated which earned him a lot of respect and also this lesson went down deep into my existence. I promised, I would not give such surprises to anyone and be very proactive in raising the alarm when I feel something is going to go nasty or fall behind schedule. Just ensure that you do not do the same mistake that I did and land your manager into such troubles. This can severely impact your performance reviews and hence the growth.

Being Polite and respectful

You should treat your manager or senior leadership the way you would like to be treated and a little more.

It's not because the managers demand that respect but they actually deserve that respect. The reason they are your manager or at any leadership position, trust me, they have earned it with effort. It rarely comes to anyone on a platter. Even if you do not feel like respecting the individual even then you need to respect the position. No one is a favourite of all - we are not at ice cream shops where we all get one of our choices!

From your viewpoint you may feel your manager does nothing but every manager irrespective of the team it leads is always wearing the burnt of all the external hostilities. It may come to him because you or one of your team members may have done something but he is answerable and handles that for you - so you need to respect that position. As a manager he is responsible to spearhead this whole team to success and it cannot happen without your support.

> *"In case your manager fails or you set him to failure trust me – you and your whole team would fall apart and lose".*

Success or failure is just a representation of how good or bad you and your team has performed so please ensure that you respect him and you never know that one day you might become the same manager and your peers with whom you have spoilt the environment may become your own liability and they may continue to treat you the way you have been treating your manager so you may end up being the undertaker for yourself.

Not only to your managers but the managers and leaders of other teams also should be treated with respect. In fact, not just these managers but each and every individual you come across, treat them with respect because how you treat them shows less about them but more about you. It's more about your personal value system that gets projected when you treat others with respect. All my life, I have been very polite, loving and respectful to everyone I met and it was invariably reciprocated. Respect is one of the basic attribute or craving that every individual has. Being Human, nobody wants to feel less important or less respected so please treat each one with respect and you would feel and see the results for yourself. Your manager will also reciprocate. Similarly in case you are not treated well you can really go back and tell your manager that this is not going well with you and ask him for guidance on what you can do to be treated differently and this will go a long way in making a successful career. In case the manager is treating everyone badly - go to his boss and ask for intervention during skip level sessions.

"Your overall demeanour determines your success. During promotions - mostly 360 reviews are done and in case you have rubbed someone in the wrong way, you never know it may catch up with you at some amazingly crucial point so simple MANTRA - Be Professional all the time"

You can take leverage only with colleagues with whom you are very close and that too with careful evaluation. Don't initiate too much of personal interference from your end - evaluate and be observant of what is the level of personalization the other person is comfortable with.

In my own organisation there were two qualified people, one of them was very brash and another one was very polite and respectful to everyone and at some point of time there was a position for one to be made a manager. The person who was more polite humble and respectful was chosen over the other person with similar skill set because it's another quality that you would like to have in your new leaders/managers.

You may be outstanding, smart, the brightest mind around but if you are not able to treat your subordinates and up above with respect you may end up being the last. Having confidence and capability is great but we need to keep in check before it becomes arrogance and nuisance.

Never Misbehave with managers/leaders

Being respectful and professional is a basic culture and shall be a no brainer. In case there is problem take proper channel to address it but do not show up as a jerk. There is a way we conduct ourself in offices.

I can quote several examples where messing up with management has resulted in only one thing. Departure or sabotage of your progress/position –

Nobody ever wins a battle against the manager

Sounds weird but this is mostly true its not boss is powerful but generally we are not looking the larger objectives. He/She is tasked to get things done with you or without you. He is also in same situation under his boss where tasked to deliver but people are manager's accountability and asset – manager is generally given a choice to get his team but team or individual rarely get to choose their managers.

There could be exceptions where manager is already infamous across the floor and organisation for being illogical, irrational or stupid. However, such situations are rare as your manager also has a manager - so we can safely assume - your boss exists because he delivered on his KPIs to organization. Managers are chosen with a lot more care and are under more scrutiny always so they are generally doing the right things. Therefore, whenever you are picking up a battle against your manager ensure that you are not the only person who is at fault or on the battle front because many a times fault is on our side and you end up blaming your boss. Generally speaking the top performers rarely have complaints for their boss – they are able to see and align themselves to their managers' objectives – be one team and get executing.

> *Please note – I am strictly against boot licking or lip services but being professional and respectful is not negotiable!!*

So don't get me wrong. I am not asking you to bend unreasonably or be scared and tolerate crap but a word of caution - *Look before you leap!*

> *One most common trait among poor performers is their animosity towards team and/or manager.*

Most of the time, they are found bitching or cribbing about the team and/or manager - not sure what comes first - team/manager do something or its just poor performers perception but it throws them into a vicious circle.

Word of Caution - Early Warning!

Whenever you find you are upset with your manager and team - it's high time you need to get to the discussion table and clear your perspectives - in no time you are going to hit poor performer grade. It's generally the starting point of demotivation and performance degradation!!!!

Manager's Mind

This is an important one – we need to understand where is Manager's mind. Learning things from his perspective is critical This is a key to being successful and sows seeds for growth. Once you start thinking from your managers perspective you will expand your thought process beyond your individual accountability and responsibilities. You may end up being someone who can understand the larger picture. This would directly help you to contribute more towards the objective your manager is chasing and once you do that you would anyways be contributing to the manager's success and your success as they are not unrelated. This is the fastest way to be managers favourite.

One off the leaders we spoke to, mentioned –

Once my boss who was VP, asked me what this job is all about? I gave all the possible answers but he summed it up

"Its making me (Manager) Successful"

Lining up with Manager's priority is so critical.

This also helps you to become part of the solution rather than being part of the problem.

Let's say your manager comes and tells the team that we are going to operate 24 × 7 from next month. Now you can present lot of resistance because you have been comfortable working in 9 to 6. However manager has to request or force your whole team to adhere to this and there is no option. This situation would bring stress to everyone. Now you may give a long list of reasons why you cannot do the night shift and then you may go around and propagate that negativity across the team so that whole team is now not ready to support this new request. With that your manager can either come to your terms and tell leadership that my team cannot do it or he may start hiring for new folks who would be ready to work in the shift. Think from the manager's perspective, about him and his failure would gradually be seen as failure of your whole team together and each one of you may lose the job so it is important that you look at things from the managers perspective and ask questions if you could not but don't assume and try to go the other side.

What manager asks for something to be done (business related)

– It has to be done.

You would do it or someone else but it has to be done. If you do it more than others you learn more and get more opportunities in future.

Collaboration and Acceptability

Collaboration and Acceptability within your team is crucial. From the perspective of senior management you should be able to gel well with your colleagues, your peers and teammates who may or may not be reporting into the same boss. You have to ensure that your manager should feel comfortable while assigning task to you knowing that you can work with all your colleagues easily. If you aspire to become a leader - you would have to build a defacto reputation that team would not mind if you are promoted as their manager. This won't come easy if team has more than one person competing to grow but still majority of your team should see you more sound for a managerial role. You will have to earn it. Unfortunately, when team has too many strong people and all trying to grow as a manager for same team - this is where leadership intervention becomes necessary to ensure team's collaboration remains intact. However, in such situations - a person who is more mature during altercations, keeps his calm, do not get into trivia fights - mostly has his way - as it appears to be a sign of maturity.

Careless Escalations

We shall ensure there are no escalations due to your carelessness

> *"You are as good as your last transaction –*
> *people have short term memory"*

so that puts a responsibility of bringing consistency and sanity to your work. Ensure to have good rapport with your customers and no trivial mistakes in your work which can be attributed to pure carelessness. One mistake can also become Achilles heel.

Carelessness is not dependable. Imagine a situation when something critical has to be done and there is an option to choose from somebody who was careless once and somebody who had been very thorough in his work. Who would you go with? Try to see - simple aspects.

Stewardship

"Stewardship - Leadership: The job of supervising or taking care of something, such as an organization or property"

While working on the upward management it is important to understand that leadership or management should have confidence that you can pick up projects/initiatives and run with it. This is extremely important as you grow in the organisation because it helps to establish a fact that you are ready for such or more complex projects or assignments. This is like a virtuous cycle, you are given a project, you succeed in it, you are given another project based on your confidence from your previous project you demonstrate great results again and a larger project is given to you and cycle continues.

Own and run with initiatives

| Think of the organization like your own mini-bread store and take actions and make decisions as you would if it were your company. | Sameer Bondre |

You should be leading your project with complete ownership and accountability where nobody should feel that they need to intervene to keep your project on track. You need to reinforce, a confidence in your leadership and management that once a task or project is assigned to you they can rest assured for its delivery and success. The very moment you are able to achieve this level of confidence you would have already secured your position for enriching learning and organisational success. This is based on my personal experience. I joined the organisation as a fresher and along with my day to day work I was part of many committees at TCS and each event or project that we did, out of my regular scope of work, did help me to grow my understanding of corporate world. It helped me to start working with personal influence rather than vested authority by the organisation. Back then, I did not have any title of a manager or a lead but since I was owning more than everybody else I was consulted more than anybody else and thus I was trusted with additional responsibilities more than anybody else. This is again a simple demonstration of how you can be a leader without being designated.

Leader by Influence

Be a leader at your level by influence. This is an interesting aspect of the organisation where not every time you would be given a designation or a title but expected to lead the project or a team. This is your opportunity to grab. I would help you with some of the fundamental concepts that help you lead without a title. As long as you are doing following you would end up being leader.

Know More than anybody else in the team

This is not to defeat or compete with anyone but to perform and lead. The person equipped with most knowledge would be in the driving seat sooner or later.

Networking

The more cross collaboration you can bring to the table would determine your position again as a leader. Let's say you are the one who is front ending the conversations with all the associated teams, like it or not you would be again in the driving seat so please focus on cross team collaboration.

Finding Common Ground

You have to keep yourself neutral and not driven with your sentiments or emotions towards one side presented by a group of people. There would be conflicting views and you have to take a neutral ground to understand both sides and then come to a conclusion that would gradually bring people to you for clarification. Let's say, there are 3 people in the team, two can't decide, only when you are on one side that decision gets done so you better keep your options open and be a free float whom both the other two can trust for being balanced and rightful.

Bold & Confident

You have to demonstrate confidence and aplomb during tricky situations. When project is going through the doldrums, you have to elevate the spirit of the group and ensure they are not giving up midway. You have to reinforce with everyone the purpose with which the project was initially triggered. Most of the time that helps to restore enthusiasm and passion. This brings back the team on track and start running again so please keep this in mind always "why this project is being done in the first place?". Do not pick up a project unless you yourself are convinced that this is worth doing. In case it's absolutely necessary to do a project then take help of your leadership and get convinced about the purpose of this project. It's important to have the conviction for a project otherwise it gets difficult to motivate team and achieve the objectives.

Brand Ambassador for your team

Try to observe - each team would have an officially designated manager and then there would be an un-official manager who would be interacting with all the other teams and in fact various teams would try to reach out to this guy in absence of the manager. Now this is what happens when you do beyond your day-to-day scope of work where you interact with other teams and you gradually become face of your team. Why do you think this is important? It is important because every small thing gets noticed. If you are interacting with various people and various teams you would gradually have more awareness about the surroundings and the organisation than any of your colleagues. That gradually brings better decision making for you when compared to the rest of the team members and you gradually turn out to be the next in command with your manager. Thankfully I enjoyed this position a lot when I was not a manager because of my peer engagement (mostly un-official and unrelated to business) that helped to weld personal relationships with people who at the end of the day helped in professional aspects.

Internalise your job..i.e. basically believe in your role and that it can make a difference to your organization and yourself	Sameer Srivastava

You will be amazed to see how non related team members who interact with you during unofficial occasions for different projects become an asset during your actual business critical situations.

For being the top performer, you have to be a brand ambassador of your team and become the second in command by interacting with different people collaborating with various teams and ensuring that you represent your team appropriately even in places where your manager is not around. Gradually, everybody should feel that you can at least give insights about your team, you may not be the decision maker but you can definitely provide the in-depth details about your function. This also means that you would have to learn about your function pretty well and be able to think by stepping into the shoes of your manager. Unless manager is of unsecure breed - he would appreciate all your support and you shall be rewarded accordingly.

Being proud of team

Positive & proud about what your team does and celebrate it often. This is an important aspect again. Try to recollect interactions that you might have had with different colleagues from different teams who always bitch about their team. Do you feel they do it just in front of you.

NO, they gradually end up talking the same thing to everyone and they bad mouth their team publicly. Trust me, nobody ever appreciate that conversation. These people are toxic and should be avoided at all cost most importantly you should not be one of them. The more positive you talk about your team it reinforces your belief in your own team and that pushes your performance. You must be proud of what your team does and then only you would be able to talk great things about the team and gradually establish a reputation for your team and yourself. You like it or not the success of your team depends again upon how it is being perceived across the other teams. This particular task cannot be completed just by your manager himself or herself but it needs a congruent effort from each of the team members. Be a team where every member is proud of it. All the top performing teams haves this basic underlying DNA exactly the same - they all are proud of what they do, the meaning they bring to the business and the outcomes they deliver to their customers. You might still have a lot of internal clashes, frictions but it's like a family fight which should "by all means" stay within the boundary of household. In case, you want to grow in your organisation and be considered as a trustworthy second in command you must without fail be positive about your team. This characteristic is sooner or later recognised by your management and rewarded as well. I was so proud of my Rockers team which involved in Corporate Social responsibility initiatives and we were able to market it so well within India leadership that when our CEO visited India I was given an opportunity to share with him all great work that we have done in India. That great opportunity came to me just because I was part of such an initiative and always felt proud of what we were doing as a team. This holds true for any team that we belong to.

Team's Capability

Being confident about your team's capability is awesome thing. Currently, you are an individual and in order to accomplish what we discussed above, you have to be confident about your team capability as well. Team is as good as its weakest player like a chain is as strong as its weakest link so it's important that we help each other to become strong to ensure that sum total strength of our team is exceptionally high. Unless you are confident about your team capability you will not be able to market it well or publicize it or talk great about it. You may sound like somebody who doesn't have a great team or it may reflect bad at yourself that you do not have confidence in your team. To bring this home, let me ask a quick question, assume you meet two people and one of them is criticizing his family and doing it with all his heart and mind while the other reflects respect, love, care and affection for his family - whom do you think you would respect more? For a while you may empathize with one who is cribbing but if you are given to choose him for any project you are driving which involve family you may not pick him up but the other guy because a dysfunctional family doesn't reflect good on anyone or any family member so it's the same logic here, if you criticize your team you are not going to be considered in a great regard by anyone so never ever try to score brownie points by talking low of your team. If you do it and your leadership comes to know about it - will do more damage than good. People who want to get to better positions instead of cribbing about what is wrong in the team focus on fixing it and making the team a great team so think whether

"you are a part of a problem or a solution - the choice is yours"

Projecting your Team

So far we agree that upward management requires us to ensure that we are the brand ambassador for our team so we need to seek opportunities where we can project our team. The initiatives organised by various teams and businesses among the organisation can serve as a wonderful platform for this purpose. At times there are competitions for innovation, coding, quality metrics etc so we should always leverage opportunities and ensure that our team is positioned as a performer. This kind of participation has more than one advantage it not only makes your team famous and position it appropriately among various leadership levels but it also serves to you an opportunity to learn and grow further. I would repeat -

please always keep in mind that any initiative being conducted in your organisation is an opportunity and should be leveraged. There is nothing to lose but win. It positions you and your team across leadership from various business units that can be super helpful for you.

Org Level Initiatives

Participate in org level initiatives. This helps you to popularize your team and yourself: in my own career I would have not learnt as much if I was limited to my own team and this holds true for all the enthusiastic colleagues I have worked with. We were not satisfied just by doing our day to day job but always looked forward to opportunity which would help us grow and learn and interestingly all of us were the top performers. I have mentioned above some interactions and networking that you do during the course of these events is like an investment into your own work because no team works in silos and when you interact or have to collaborate with various teams such interactions which you have had during the course of initiatives go a long way. Once you go and perform in such initiatives and win laurels for you team, even your management projects it to external teams and leadership which in turn helps you to shine as an individual and team gets an opportunity to be rewarded for all the good work. The important message here is to work hard - ensuring that you have your personal recognition as well as your team is recognised for all the good work.

Technological competence

Learning all that your team has to offer: now this is another very important aspect of being a top performer and is very helpful in upward management also. I didn't realise the importance of this aspect at the beginning of my career and no wonder I had a poor beginning. What I have come to believe that you are always respected for your knowledge. People may like you - people may not like you but they cannot ignore your knowledge. Your importance for position, job security and performance all are largely dependent on your technical acumen. As long as you are in technical job and when I say technical it doesn't mean only the scripting languages but the knowledge of what you do, the involved processes, the criticality of the interactions etcetera...so if you want to ensure that your manager likes you or at least is dependent on you, you need to be technically sound and be able to demonstrate the same thing to him as well.

Spend time in learning and learning thoroughly. There was a time when I joined a team "Release Management". I joined as one of the fresher and I had very senior people in the team. Just because of my curiosity within one year I was able to learn all the three roles that my team had to offer and that insured I was a Top performer or an outperformer because I can actually perform all the roles that were required by the management or this team. This also helped me to become one of the youngest managers in my organisation because I was technically sound, I knew all my processes and also I had a good reputation across the teams which helped me to drive my team more effectively. This gave me a very solid foundation and strong starting point on my management journey. Even after becoming the manager, I was valued by team because I was able to do each and everything that any of my reportee could do. Even if you are a manager it is important to learn the basics of what your team does. A 30 thousand feet manager is not very effective so be very careful of that. In summary, be the go to guy for your manager because of your technical competence.

Business/Functional Competence

Be a person who can talk about all the aspects of business. In case, anybody wants to know anything about your team you should be the person whom they would like to reach out to. That means you have to have a solid foundation of business, the decision making strategies and Technical delivery. If you don't know please spend some time with your manager and learn till a level where your manager feels comfortable putting you as his backup.

Availability

A call away: Not many times you would receive calls from your team, generally you would unless you're completely useless. Person who is never called out of his shift is generally not very valuable this is an unofficial benchmark - at times you can use this to evaluate your own position in the team. Another important aspect to observe here is that not all the managers would disturb you unless it is critical and thus whenever you receive a call from your manager you should immediately pick it up or do a call back... now this is absolutely not necessary to be done in case you do not want to grow or be a top performer. Let's say you are the strongest person a manager has got but whenever required you are not available you may not go a very long way within your organisation. I have worked with at least two technically outstanding resources but you cannot trust them for their availability it's like you have a nuclear missile but you don't know if it will shoot during the war or not that way it defeats the purpose of having such a weapon. So if you have to matter and your technical skill set to be respected and used please ensure your availability so that manager is not left in dilemma whether his phone would be answered or not whether you'd be available or not.. Must do for every performer ensure that you are available for the team.

Call back for missed call: This is a very simple yet many times taken for granted. In case you see a missed call by a manager or a team or family member please call them back you never know what you may be able to fix. Same goes with the SMS text as well. Please ensure that any sms or text responded well in time.

I understand time is changing. Orgs are moving towards NO DISTURBANCE policies – where people are not bothered beyond their shifts but in case its required – do support.

Manager's Alignment

Acting with managers backing and awareness is very important to ensure you are not surprising him and getting surprised in return.

"Never take bold steps without your manager's awareness so that you are not asked to retreat"

This is really important folks. By all means secure management approval before acting or making some big strides,

Do not surprise your manager because you'd be surprised by the outcome.

I have seen situations where worst of the projects and mistakes have been tackled very effectively because the manager was aligned and I have also seen where a small mistake has blown Up Out Of proportion because manager chose to screw up the miscreant just to teach a lesson or set an example.

On every project where you want to push stuff through the team its again important - There have been multiple occasions where you and I want to do something and face resistance from team in rolling it out. Disability or inability to run a project can cost you dearly. The trick here is to ensure that your manager is aware of your project and you have his or her buy in to do it. Once you have alignment from your manager your team will follow through and chances of success with the project would increase manifold. It also helps to secure all the resources like people or budget is made available to you and you can set up sail for a successful journey.

Chapter 6

DOWNWARD MANAGEMENT

Have an aim to become a good leader than manager rest will follow	Ravi Mylariah

Downward management means how you tackle your subordinates or people who report into you. This is equally important to grow in your career and their performance. If you are a manager, your success will depend on the performance of your team and in case the team fails to perform eventually you fail to perform so it becomes extremely important for you to focus on the performance of your team. I would cover a few basic aspects you should be mindful of while interacting with your subordinates and this is about the mindset than anything else. The most important underlying concept manager has to be seen as fair, solution oriented and a mature balanced individual.

Let's get started and review some of the game rules that would help us to set compass in the right direction.

Respect your team members

you will only reap what you sow so if you want to be respected then you should better be respectful toward your colleagues, reports, and your boss. You don't have a choice but have to be respect full:) This is a very old thought process where team members were treated like not equals. Time has changed. In large and structured organisation you could easily get a HR escalation for mistreating employee. Better harness & create relationship by maintaining mutual respect. This is something I learnt while working with Avaya, it has one of the best culture in the world.

I was surprised when senior most leaders used to come to us while we were engineers and used to treat us as equals. They never differentiated between an engineer or manager or senior manager or leader. That helped me and all the other top performing managers to grow with the similar value system and we ensured that we propagated the same. Eventually the overall culture that we create is of a mutual respect that ensures better eSAT and cSAT. Such environment makes everyone contribute more.

Treat with fairness/equality

What are 5 MUST NOT DOs for anyone who want to be successful ? - Never miss on Ethics. - Don't repeat same mistakes. - Fail fast and come out of it. In case you are repeating failures – you won't succeed. Learn Fast. - Don't Create politics, silos, and make unhealthy environment and division. No Bias – No nepotism as a leader.	Gerald Wilson

Fairness and equality is not negotiable. you cannot be a great manager unless you can demonstrate neutrality. Manager who is not neutral may not be able to run a very effective team because team won't have confidence in the person. What irritates the most is when the decision maker is biased. Team feels there is no hope for them against favouritism. To handle this, we need to demonstrate a great consistent character. Do whatever it takes to ensure that team believes in you to take an unbiased decision. Establish that and anybody can get the beating and anybody can get the appreciation based on the merit of the case. The decision won't be biased because of favouritism or nepotism. At times you may have to publicly criticize everyone together so that no one feels only he or she is at the receiving end. Do not delay in acting against complaints because

your words are as good as your actions

There was a time when I was managing a group of Technical managers and they were just a handful now since each one of them did not have visibility to what other is doing, they were frustrated assuming that each one of them is doing more than the other and they were surprised why I am not bashing or penalizing others. I always tried to show each one of them what value others were bringing to the table but in spite of all my efforts I really wasn't able to make it as a completely collaborative team. In such cases the maturity of the individual would also matter and based on their individual maturity they would be able to see the situation from your perspective but never the less you should give your best to ensure that you treat all of them still the same and not get biased with anything that is fed to you by others.

As a manager at times you may get too much information from so many people with good and bad intentions, where people want to exploit your position to their benefit so always be mindful before you act. Do compare all the things that you have got to know after reducing the emotional content from that and once you are sure that you understand what is done and the intent why it is done then only act on it. Trust me it can be daunting and confusing.

Always Remember and Ask this to yourself

> *"What if two parties or people appearing to you as in conflict - are just playing that in front of you"*

This would make you take more balanced decision. This is especially true when in highly politicized and emotionally driven environment.

Trust your Teammates

You need to trust your team and reportee. For this, firstly you will have to grow, build courage and confidence in yourself. Once you are strong and planted you can extend the comfort to team and let them play, explore and grow in the process.

Let me quote an example

My first switch of job was unique in its own way - Jumped off from being a mainframe software developer to an AVAYA Product support engineer. I lost 3 years of work ex and started from zero as professionally both streams were quite different. At that time I was thinking what a bold decision I took. However, years later when I grew into a manager myself - I reflected that while I made that choice 2 people - trusted me, showed more courage, management grit and confidence than me. They are my first manager Adarsh Mudugere and back then Senior Manager - Anurag Bahadur. They certainly did their evaluation for basic fitment and gave me a ground to explore and deliver. I realized how important it is for a management team to have that level of trust on team members and a self-confidence to act as a catch net if the person fails. Adarsh always gave me a free hand to work on my day to day job and participate in anything that I wanted to do while Anurag trusted me with a big responsibility to handle our yearly event. He always came across as a mentor / guide and a guardian who was self-assured; he can take care of things if I or the team fails/run into challenges. We always had great events under his leadership - just to add this was not his day job. While he was leaving AVAYA we were concerned and worried as we were losing a strong leader but he quoted.

"I see Madhup and you folks will take up and a new breed of leaders will emerge" that trust is so inspiring. He was right - Madhup became Site Head of Avaya-HP in Pune and when he left I was made the Site Head. That's what a leader does to you. Invests trust in you and you are committed to grow and deliver on that trust. It's a trait of a great leader. Like his confidence helped us become better and be more useful to the org - you can also demonstrate that trust and help folks grow!

Pay for performance

This was the first lesson I learnt after becoming a manager. It was my first performance review and I got some money to distribute within my team and I being a great humble/generous soul I actually assigned everyone more or less equal percentage of money so that I am rewarding my team consistently and unbiased. When I presented this to my manager Adarsh he was surprised and asked me a question

"Are you not being unfair to people who have worked up and beyond for business compared to others who did ONLY what was expected?"

That day I was deeply touched and realised how unfair you could be by being too neutral. Since that day I always ensured that anybody who has performed more than the other get paid accordingly or rewarded accordingly. I gradually inculcated the same value system in my organisation and all the managers who were reporting into me. Everybody in my organisation knew that they would be treated fairly and they would be rewarded for their performance which eventually improved the performance of the team.

Be consistent and predictable

Imagine a manager who is very polite one day, shouting another day and you are left guessing what is exactly going on in the mind of this manager. This creates a sense of insecurity and reflects poorly on the manager because at some degree it reflects the lack of decisiveness. When I say you have to be predictable that means you should have said clearly to your team that what all behaviours would be appreciated and which behaviours would not be tolerated. This outlines and establishes the culture of your team.

"Clarity is Power"

Please be clear about the culture yourself and do communicate the same to the team to ensure consistency from top to bottom. Let's say you are allowing work from home for your team members, here the team should have a clear understanding preferably as a written documentation which advices - in what all conditions work from home would be allowed and in which conditions it would be rejected. That way you would never get accused of being favourable to some people and not so accommodating for others.

Please standardise anything and everything that may lie in the grey area and lead to conflicts.

Logically no nonsense guy

There is a difference between a nice manager and a stupid manager. You can be very nice and yet fool proof. At any point of time your team should not get a sense that you would take any shit. I don't mean that you become offensive and start misbehaving with the team just to prove that you are not a nice guy and a very strict manager but everyone in the organisation needs a manager; let me stress this everybody within the organisation needs a manager. You might be very good with the team, very open, generally approachable and more like a friend but you need to ensure that at some degree your team understands that you are the manager. Also, in case you become too friendly you might end up losing on your operations and team starts taking you for granted. Thus, be very mindful of that.

Not everyone is worth your openness

Because of prevailing immaturity in certain individuals as soon as you get very close to them they would start feeling like they can take you for granted which would eventually hurt you because the mature people would appreciate your openness and still respect your position. However, immature people would jump onto a conclusion that you are as good as their colleagues and your deliveries may not get the priority they deserve. Be mindful of this fact *"Not everyone is worth your Openness"*

Feedback

This is a great tool that can make or break your organisation. Feedback would be positive or negative based on the circumstances and situation. There is an old saying –

appreciate in public and criticize in private.

Feedback should never be generic. It should always have facts/examples to elaborate on and to explain to the individual how the things have impacted or at least were perceived from your perspective or the leadership standpoint. Nobody wants to make a mistake or goof up things but it just happens, so once they get an opportunity to rectify themselves there is a good chance that they would take away the lesson and build on it for any future interactions or situations.

Always give constructive feedback and give people a chance & direction to learn and grow. It should always be forward looking rather than backward looking.

Before you give feedback, first understand the individual motivation and trigger points and based on those personal motivations, plan your feedback as you know to get something done you need to put fire in the heart of the person - which can only be done once you hit the right chords. With any team member I work with I generally know the trigger points. I

spend time to understand what motivates each individual

and then only device my strategy to help them achieve their own inclinations, targets, aspirations and on the way they shall accomplish what organisation is trying to accomplish with this individual. There are rarely contradictory or conflicting interests between an individual and the organisation and its upto the manager to figure out the mapping. The key is to put the right person for the right job and this is impossible unless you have spent time to understand the individual. I can't stress enough on this. I would really request each one of you to spend a great amount of time in learning about your team members before delegating or engaging them into any task.

Building unity

Building Unity is essential to be a common agenda of the team.

"All for one and one for all"

Back in AVAYA there used to be a team where each of the team members were outstanding. They all were technically very strong, they knew their job very well. Most importantly they stood by each other during thick and thin. It was always a pleasure working with the team because you can sense the love the team had for each other. It was one of the top performing team. As a manager if there is a lot of infighting going on within your team it would be increasingly difficult for you to manage that team and deliver any meaningful results. So, in order to ensure that such non-productive things do not take away your bandwidth and you better invest some time to proactively address any of the teething issues regarding the teamwork, unity or overall team behaviour.

Now the question is how you go about it - you might have to take small steps first like

- Reward the uniting behaviour.
- In all your meetings, put team results above individual contribution.
- Nip conflicts in the bud - do not let them grow into Banyan trees.
- Go for Outings and engage in activities where you play and win as a team. Cricket / Football matches also can do the trick.

Building sense of pride in team

Building sense of pride in team is important because nobody wants to be associated with losers. There must be a dignity and respect that you demonstrate for your team. Only once you are successful in making your team damn proud of what it does you would also see their interaction would increase or become better with the other teams and the organisation. In any communication, your position matters and how you would be treated or how you would treat others - so a team member who belongs to a team for which he is already proud of, he would most likely dominate the conversations and you would be able to harness this advantage to get better propositions/negotiations for the team. Thus, there has to be a structured effort in order to ensure that this spirit percolates down to each team member because we are as good as our weakest link of the chain. Let me quote an example - when I joined TCS Mumbai Yantra Park Thane, I was part of shipping and billing team in a project for IMP. After sometime, I realised and naturally felt that my team which was a 3 member team was one of the best and I unknowingly kept on branding incessantly that my team is the best. I kind of seeded that thought in mind of other two Team members as well. We realised that we were living to very *high standards ourselves* and even management saw us differently. We enjoyed good ratings, zero escalations and a wonderful working environment. While I left the team our team lead told me, before I joined the team they were still performing well but they never felt so proud of what they did. They never thought we can matter so much. Since, I joined the team and started talking high of our team, it influenced others as well. We just didn't feel that way but delivered accordingly. We were recognized by our management as well. I still believe and feel very happy that we were the best:):)

This is something you would feel naturally once you compare your contributions in a positive light, more often every other team can say they are big deal, doing the toughest work in the world but the litmus test for this proposition is whether each and every member of your team works hard to maintain those high standards. When your team works together towards this common goal of keeping your team as Number 1, where they can put team before themselves and rejoice the accomplishment as a team rather than an individual then you can conclude that yes your team has achieved this unity and you are all set for great performance together!

Capability is a prime focus

I have mentioned this earlier as well that capability is the foremost and the non-negotiable. When it comes to your downward management and you are not able to groom your team technically or from process standpoint, your team would never have the required confidence to outshine the competition. This is the most important inherent value that we need to develop as managers to ensure that organisation continue to value your team. Unless you develop capabilities which are unique, your team can perish because some other team, some other company might be able to do the same job much cheaper so we need to keep that competitive as a manager and in order to accomplish that capability development is the most powerful weapon in the arsenal.

How do we go around making this as a value or culture?

Start rewarding people who are going the extra mile to learn and accomplish more. Invariably in each one on one that you set up with your team members begin with the discussion what did they learn since your last conversation till now and in case there is a roundabout answer stop there and ask them to either go back to learn something new and come back tomorrow or warn them that by next meeting you should have done/learn something which you don't know currently. This way in each one on one with every individual of your team you would be pushing Inch By Inch your team to completely different level of capabilities. Sum Total of your team's capability would shoot up phenomenally.

Challenge your team regularly with more and more complex tasks.

Ask them questions which force them to get deeper next level – at least ask 3 Whys if not 5.

You would realize, your team would start getting deeper on all interactions.

Think and answer it for yourself the kind of reward you can reap by having a technically outstanding team. One reward I can tell you for sure as you won't have to get involved in small issues and team would be able to take care of most of these challenges by themselves and only quality escalations would come to you. Ponder over that thought and start devising your strategy towards this important aspect of capability development.

Metrics management

"What gets measured can be managed"
&
"What gets monitored, gets done"

These two statements highlight the importance of metrics management. We need to identify the key metrics that we should observe from Operations standpoint and once we have identified those metrics we need to inform the team the significance of each one of them and how they would be kept intact. Let's say there is a customer related SLA over the closure time of the case. We need to help them understand why it is important not for our organisation but for the customer as well. It is observed when people understand the purpose of what they are doing then they are able to deliver better on that. Many a times management feels that this is too much of a detail to be passed on to the front line resources. To me that's not a right idea unless there is some confidentiality involved. I would recommend all the managers to share the WHYs before you share the HOWs.

Promoting collaboration

Collaboration is something that flows from top down and we have to build a culture of such collaboration. This collaboration shouldn't be limited to our own team internally but it should go beyond and should be extended to other teams and all stakeholders we come across. At times it becomes even difficult to collaborate with non-supportive team members internally and externally and that's where the trick is.

Let me give you an example, while I was managing Technical Voice operations for Vodafone Idea Contact Centres - One day there was an issue with Assam region and I went to check with network team and asked them are you guys working on this? One of the team member immediately started giving me another set of questions like "Do you know what the problem is?", "Do you know who should you be working on this", "Do you know if it is a problem with the link or with the system itself" etc... honestly the answer could have been simple "NO" and if there was a knowledge gap it could have been politely conveyed that it's not a network issue. I realised that the intent was not of a collaboration but to prove that one team is better than the other or maybe I don't know the basic things. By then I had matured enough in that kind of environment to handle this. I gave it back to some extent and went back to my desk. I was dejected, pissed and felt so sorry about the lack of collaboration among the closely working teams. When the senior members of the team are behaving like this what kind of culture would be at the junior level. As a manager, it should be our responsibility to ensure that all the teams stand together and also extend every possible support to anybody who comes to us for help. Once you treat others well you can (not 100% of times) rest assured to get similar feeling and affection back when you need it. There would be exceptions but still percentage would be ignorable or very low. To the contrary if we work hard on fault finding and wasting our energy in pulling each other down, no one succeeds. It's gross.

Please promote cooperation by all means and reward it to get repeated!

Advantages of cooperation go long way

- Quick Turnarounds.
- Happy Working Culture.
- Avoided Blame Game when things go wrong.
- Happy Customers and Employees.

When you move to Director and above levels – this gets more and more serious. You cannot climb up the ladders unless you can collaborate.

Empathy

*"If you can't empathize, you can't be a great leader.
Because people are emotions"*

While growing up as a manager there have been so many times when I wanted to put employee needs before business preferences. Now this is a tricky part if you compromise business for your employees, gradually, you will end up compromising your employees for business.... please reread.. if you compromise business for employees gradually you will end up compromising your employees for business.

If you don't have business you don't have employees and you have to let these employees go. At the same time you cannot ignore the employees completely where they are cribbing, feeling grumpy, are agitated, demotivated and disappointed. Even in such scenarios you are bound to fail. This becomes more of a balancing act where you are making decisions which are not completely one sided.

There was a situation when we have to call people to work from home because of business needs and people readily agreed. They did compromise their personal vacations and week off to continue to support the operations from their home. Eventually, there were situations when team members wanted to work from home because they had something to take care at home while they can still support business to large extent from home. We agreed and we gradually allowed people to work from home. The underlying thought in my mind was, team works for the business at the personal time so at times we may give an option for these folks to work from home to provide a good working environment. Team also insured that the work was not hampered while they are working from home.. gradually we realised that few people are taking work from home much more than the others and to an extent where some people even don't work while they say they are working from home. Soon we realised that we have people working from home even without informing us, some of them who were based out of remote locations. This generated a sense of insecurity and partiality among the hard working people and that was unacceptable. We had to take some strong measures to stop this practice of work from home. That wasn't easy either and we had to face lot of resistance. Gradually, we reduced the work from home and it would be only given if business needs and otherwise there is no work from home policy. We were never very strict to deploy this because our team really gave every bit they could to ensure the work is done properly so it always remained mutual - we as a team wanted to do it differently but we maintain status quo and that worked out really ok.

I will tell you another story, my wife had just got operated for delivery of our first baby. She was being brought out of the operation theatre and shifted to a private room. No sooner than she was shifted, I got a call from the office and I was on a conference call from the balcony of the hospital for almost 1 hour. Thanks to family members who took care of the new-born and my wife. Do you think I was upset are concerned or cribbed around it - NO. In fact, nobody knew on that call that I was in a hospital. Almost 3 years later, I was telling this situation to one of our senior manager *Wasi Abidi* - He was deeply touched and felt really bad for me and said it was a failure of my previous manager that he should have taken care of it and you should have not got that call. I knew my manager wasn't at fault as he had no clue of that call anyways.

At times you won't realise what you are sacrificing as an employee. At times you even don't tell to your manager and this generally happens with the top performers but see the impression that *Wasi* demonstrated - made me feel - this is a level of empathy I also should carry and no wonder Wasi has been so famous among his team members and always loved by his team. I learnt this lesson from him and I always ensure that any of my team member if he is going through any personal emergency or crisis I move earth and heaven to ensure that I provide all the possible comfort to the employee the word is "always".

Let me quote another story - at times you find highly motivated employees and I would like to share one of my ever favourite team member - Ameer. He was one of my most dependable team members if something is given to him you would only get results nothing less. He would compromise, his life, his family's happiness or anything in front of business. He would do this voluntarily and you will not even know what all he has compromised.

There was a situation where his daughter was having fever of 104 admitted in hospital and from there he was working. As soon as I realise that he was working from the hospital in this situation immediately asked him to stop that - he said daughter is sleeping and I have nothing to do so I just thought I'll work. Such kind of human beings who believe their work to be their prayer are found rarely - they are God's gift to organisations though the family may not think the same way. It's important to drive balance but I can tell you that such efforts are also rewarded and when we got the chance we really did whatever we could do for him to make his transition to a different company & country seamless. Right from me to the senior most management we had access to - knew Aamir, his commitment and we all did our best to return the favour which he earnestly deserved.

Commitment and attitude is the key to success.	*Ambrish Sharma*

Another example that I came through:

There was a situation when we realised that we would have to let go of one person if not immediately but at some point in future. I called up that person at the first opportunity and conveyed the information that he should start looking out because he had a small kid and I could imagine the plight it would cause if we have to take that decision. Thankfully I never had to take that decision and the gentleman got a great opportunity somewhere outside the organisation by himself.

These examples quoted above from my personal experience are just to highlight how important it is to be able to empathize when you are a manager. Nobody gives you as a part of your job description of a manager that you have to empathize but still that's an unsaid expectation we should honor that for our own success as managers.

As a manager you would always have people cribbing about you, blaming you, pointing fingers at you and that is part and parcel of the role but deep inside your heart and mind you should know that you have been impartial, fair and kind hearted with everyone. In order to accomplish this you need to empathize and without that it would be very difficult to drive your people to the peak performance.

Communication with Your team

Hearing even what was not said: Your engineers or teammates who report into you feel that you have all the knowledge and might to manage the functions. They look up to you with lot of respect and expectations. Even if you are doing wrong they may take a lot before they are able to voice their frustrations. Rarely people walk up to the manager and tell them that they are doing it wrong but managers being human can be mistaken and go wrong so personally be open for feedback and never penalize a person for giving you such feedback. Trust me he would have mustered a lot of courage to tell you what he is telling. Some people find it easy to talk and some people find it difficult to talk to their managers about their expectations and situations so please be very mindful of such gaps that may unknowingly creep in your operations. Many a times team members feel that manager would have observed, manager would have seen, manager would acknowledge but to their surprise we fail. You don't want to but we just happen to be managing so many things that at times it falls between the cracks which team sets in a feeling of you being partial as you are noticing things partially. So, always be very careful whatever communication comes in from your team members be it oral/verbal/written or maybe even through grapevine but be very careful and cautious for any such communication that happens to reach you because you are the only person to whom your team can go to. If they start going to your boss you won't like it and even the solution would never be a Win-Win because you might not be able to appreciate the approach as much - after years of experience it won't be an issue but when you are a new manager - it can be devastating for you. It would be great if you are not that sort of a manager but I have seen several managers who take it very personally when the teammates skip a level as some managers who were reporting into me demonstrated this in a subtle way. Be very focused to any and every communication that's going around, be sensitive around it don't let it appear like fallen on deaf ears. The moment team is convinced nothing is going to change by telling things to you they would stop bringing things to you. You would lose an opportunity to help the team and yourself.

You would always be as good as your team.

If your team is respected everywhere you are respected everywhere if your team is criticized everywhere you are criticized everywhere as simple as that. However, whatever level of your brilliance maybe but if you fail to project your team appropriately you would still be considered a failure. There are many forums where only you have access to, your team members are not there in those forums and you are trusted with all the information with you. In fact they trust all the information with you and leave it to your discretion to use it for the benefit of the team. Now, imagine a situation where you are going from meetings to meetings with senior members of the leadership or higher management but you never speak up for your team, you never showcase their great work. You never showcase what accomplishments your team has - your team would be considered as an average or a laggard. In case there happens to be a colleague like one of my very highly regarded managers - he would appreciate or project his teams efforts and accomplishments (all in the right spirit) that your team work can look even dimmer so ensuring your team's efforts get the right kind of visibility is very important.

There is a brilliant example of one of the teams that I was part of The release management team. While Adarsh was leading it - we were one of the top performing teams getting kudos from every stakeholder leading several initiatives and innovation. We had a brand for ourselves. At some point of time when he left the team, the team gradually slipped into the position where it failed to enjoy the visibility it used to have earlier and gradually any misses or slippages from the team were published in a very wrong light while similar situations were treated differently earlier because of the associated perception and branding we used to enjoy. So branding of a team and perception is your responsibility and you better not fail at it. We just can't afford.

"Do not leave your reputation to chance or gossip; it is your life's artwork, and you must craft it, hone it, and display it with the care of an artist."

– Robert Greene

Here onwards whenever you get an opportunity with anyone do not miss in promoting your team's capability and accomplishments and you would reap the rewards in great proportions.

Mind it - the idea is not to show other teams down but to ensure your team efforts are presented in right light and might!

"You are the marketer of your team - they don't have anyone else to go to"
You are their only hope so ensure you do your job well.

High Standards for self and others

You look at a Maruti and Audi you know the difference you know the cost difference you know what to expect while you're stepping into Maruti and Audi. Both are cars but they are targeted for different segment and thus they have different appeal however if everybody was able to afford Audi most likely people would have gone for Audi instead of Maruti. Similarly you can either be Maruti or Audi based on the customer segment you are dealing with because the sale of Maruti cannot happen to the customer segment of Audi and similarly the Audi people may not go for Maruti. Question is who is the customer and surprisingly the customer here is yourself and your team. No one really says that they want outstanding Quality in every transaction but it is definitely an underlying expectation.

Now when you start maintaining high standards for yourself and others gradually you will see that the performance of the team is remarkable. Let's say you want meetings to start on time and everybody be punctual so it would start from you if you are not on time for Meetings nobody else would be. Unless you are doing your work in timely manner - it's unlikely that your team members would do the work in a timely manner.

One of our senior managers Murali Nayak, is an excellent example of walk the talk. He is so punctual to all his meetings that his team members don't have a choice but to be punctual. One of his team mate happens to be my very close friend and unfortunately he is very punctual that forces me also to be punctual. I never happened to be directly part of Murali's team but I end up being punctual because of his value system which was indirectly passed on to me or indirectly impacts me(for good).

One value or a high standard I would like to recommend here is – going deeper.

For technical delivery/troubleshooting we should not stop at the first answer and keep going deeper and deeper. It helps you establish a sound understanding of basic concepts and gradually you grown into an expert. Once you have established dominance over the topic gradually you start expecting the same from your team members or at least to guide them to become experts themselves. This puts everything into a Virtuous cycle and sooner or later the whole team raises the standard to entirely next level.

Chapter 7

ENSURING EMPLOYABILITY

Days of loyalty are gone. Neither employees want to stick around in the organisations for very long and nor the team rewards appropriately for the loyalty. I am generalizing this and not talking about corner cases where people are growing with regular pay hikes. It's rare except for handful growing orgs. You are as good as your current performance/appraisal cycle. You may have been the stellar performer in the past but for whatever reason personal or professional if you are not able to perform you can we on the line of fire anytime soon. I believe it's a big stupidity to leave the most important part of your life which is your earning or the family wellbeing at the mercy of your organisation. I may sound someone talking against the org but that's not what I mean. What I am referring to here is the darker side of corporate. Have fired folks have hired folks and have done several performance review so rest assured I know what I am talking about. I am not advising you to feel demotivated and start having agnostic thought process for your team and Organisation but at the same time I want you to sincerely think and ponder - what if something goes wrong with your current team, the project is scrapped or simply you are let go because of company or individual performance issues. How would you pay your next electricity bill, the gas connection, child bus fare, education fees, groceries, the expensive vacations and nevertheless all your EMIs.

That is why it is important that we take ownership of our employability. It's not just about if your company is going southwards but there might be a situation where you are not very happy with the circumstances around you in the company at that point of time also you may want to hand the boots. Instead of cribbing and getting frustrated its always advisable to move on.

I never operated so far in my career under the fear of losing the job but I've seen people who are driven with that risk. They tend to have much higher level of frustration and their decisions are more than often webbed. They lack clarity and many a times their decisions are solely based on a single agenda of saving the job. Such people suck and do no good to team or org or themselves. Insecurities run so high that team spirit is off the window very next morning.

Based on the thoughts shared above I would really like to bring on some important things that you can do to ensure that you are not completely dependent on your current job. This has a cascading effect on the family so you better take it as seriously as you could.

Learning new things

Learning new things relevant to changing market conditions is essential and non-negotiable. Long time ago if you have mastered one programming skill you would have lived your life pretty comfortably. Now with the speed of changing technologies, improvements and updates coming in the existing languages when we talk about coding it makes it absolutely necessary to continue to learn.

We have to take a closer look on how the market is shaping right now. We are moving aggressively from people driven environment to robots or pods driven environment. From on premise solution to cloud solutions. Most of the things that you could do today or are doing today in less than 5 years now will get automated so unless you are adapting to the changing Technologies and keeping yourself up to date with the latest trends you would eventually lose out.

Sometime back there used to be a dedicated Call Centre to help you book taxi and Cabs but with Ola, Uber coming in hundreds of people lost their job in the matter of few months. It was not completely their mistake they were doing their work very diligently but there has been erosion right under their feet and sooner thing can happen to us if we fail to realise the change of tide. Please spend some time on a weekly basis to identify what are your strengths, weaknesses and evaluate it against the growing market condition. You need not to get into a panic mode right away but if you're working on any archaic technology switch to a latest one and for that if you need to invest in yourself please do it. For example today Cloud Computing, Cyber security, Genetics, Automation, iot, data Analytics are some of the Hot areas for the current market. Please do your own analysis and find the skill that you are interested in and kindly persuade to mastery.

Growing with years of experience

Grow with experience and not just do the treadmill.

Don't run on treadmill when it comes to your job. Its ok you will become excellent at the same system. Now, as new generation is catching up fast they may technically outshine you and hiring manager may find him cheaper and equally capable - the less experience may get hired while you may be parked. Knowing your systems for 10+ or 20+ years won't help if your foundational learning is limited. Your systems cease to exist outside your org. So if you love your org and want to stay long enough - that is fine but then you have to be moving at least horizontally or vertically within the organisation. In case that has also not happened, it will poorly reflect on you - it could be tagged as your comfort zone and someone who is happy to be mediocre. Unfortunately, world has moved ahead of mediocre long time ago. Race is now among the aggressive, bold, confident and knowledgeable.

Salary High or Low?

Salary high or low both could be problematic. There is an interesting situation that people will rate your performance, capability and success based on your salary. How much are your earning? In case your current salary is low people might feel you might have done something wrong or your profile would have been not that great and that is why you are at such a low package. In case you happen to have a higher package most of the time the hiring manager may not be able to hire in case your package is creating a discrepancy at the team level or there are budget constraints. Now if you want to go as a Director in a company and for whatever reason your current salary happens to be that of an engineer or an entry level manager - It would be extremely difficult for you to explain your candidature for the given position. So having low salary can also cause you a great job and having a high salary also cost you a job opportunity so I would prefer to have a higher salary:)

Trick here is - Keep asking. There are good number of people who do not ask for hikes and in general end up not getting hikes as well. Manager when hard pressed with budget would generally try to bring down the noise and nuisance - meek and docile folks generally are kept to be considered when there is something extra - manager would cater to someone who has been incessantly asking for hike as this person could be an attrition risk or become demotivated low performers.

Thus you may like it or not like it - please ask for hike as appropriate. One word of caution - first deserve then demand!!

> *"Do not be a stupid - who sucks when it comes to work and asks for a great hike"*

In case you are on my team – rest assured – I will consider pay for performance and won't give in for nagging :P

When to start looking out?

There is no ideal time to start looking out. Guess you are having any of the below experiences it's time to move on.

Feels Cheated

Feeling that you have been cheated and others are being promoted ahead of you or are given better salary hikes than yourself. I am not saying that you are right in that thought process but your reality is shaped based on what you are thinking. Maybe from management standpoint they have been very fair to you and rest of the team but that doesn't matter as long as you are not happy and satisfied. The moment you feel such negative feelings are popping up - which will sooner or later start impacting your work, your work life balance and overall mental health, it is better to start looking out. Nevertheless you can talk to your manager, help him understand your frustrations and your side of story but more than often I've seen that these decisions are unchangeable because they are mostly based on lot of due diligence. Every manager who does some budget allocation for these decisions invariably does a detailed homework and can justify his or her decision. Not only at his level but his or her boss has also evaluated the decision so you can rest assured that there is not a great opportunity of change or a window of change available. In summary please give a heads up to your boss maybe to his boss as well but start looking out.

Top of the game

You know your work like the back of your hand: The moment you start feeling that everybody comes to you for answers, you are able to deal with your day today work without any problems, even in the middle of the night if somebody asks - you would be able to give them the right direction I think that's the time again to move on unless within your team or organisation you are given something to work on which is new to you. Doing a repeated task over and over again doesn't make sense if you are a career oriented person. Please start thinking abnout change!! Maybe within your function, outside the function or even outside the organisation. I know some people might feel that after so much of hard work I have earned and developed this mastery then why Prashant is suggesting to let go while I have reached a position where I can reap the benefits of my position and knowledge. I don't deny that, it is a great position to be and you would have a better job security, work-life balance, less stress but you would end up losing out on the learning that would come through if you continue to involve and engage yourself into different challenges. Unless you are growing you are dying so better be cognizant of the fact.

Falling Heads

Headcount reduction has become a need of hour and easily executed in orgs: Nobody is spared. in case you feel your position is very strong but still start searching out because that's a decay culture of an org - maybe it's because the org has cost pressures and to be profitable they have to regularly cut slack. I agree that at times it is important to do headcount reduction but if it is happening once in a while is fine but if it's happening on a quarterly basis, there's no point in staying with such an organisation. don't delude yourself.

Helpless

Helplessness: as a manager the moment you feel your own organisation is not supporting you through your most of the decisions, though you are doing great things for your customers or reporting team members then again it's a clarion call to move on because such place will not help you become a great manager or be able to deliver great results. I don't want you to pack up your bags the very day you realise that things are hopeless or there is helplessness. Talk to your management team give them a clear understanding of what you are going through and then based on the response you can make your choice whether you want to stay or move on.

Cribbing & Complaining

You find yourself Negative/Cribbing or Complaining: For whatever reason if you are feeling negative or feel like cribbing and backbiting all the time, that is also an indicator that now it's time to move on. Like all the other situations above please ensure that you inform your manager proactively, discuss the situation with him or her and then gradually move on if things do not improve. there's no point in staying in an organisation and mutilating the environment. It's nice and great to be together, try to fix things but then at some point of time you have to draw a line when things fail to improve. The best thing is to move on so that you end in the right note and don't burn the bridges where you cannot come back. Not always your manager or the organisation is at fault. At times the situation is beyond the control of your management as well. In case you cannot be part of a solution do not be a part of a problem at least. Try to help the situation if you could that's well and good. Try to improve things, collaborate with your managers, try to improve things but at any point you conclude that you may end up being a crib - that's a clarion call to start looking out.

Chapter 8

INTERVIEWS

Interviews can be looked at from two perspectives - one for hiring and another one for getting hired. Here the focus is about getting hired rather than hiring. Why I am writing on this topic of interviews? For two reasons. One I believe we should always be market ready and secondly I have cleared almost all the interviews I have participated in except for one that was for National Defence Academy. I want to share the best practices which may help you crack the interviews. It's needless to say how important it is to be able to crack the interviews in today's time. Please do not limit yourself only to this section of this book for your preparation of interviews but yes this could help you to do reasonably good and skip some basic traps.

Why we shall keep evaluating ourselves with interviews?

One of my friend Devesh Rai at the start of his career he used to change his company every 6 to 12 months. I asked him how he was so successful in cracking these many interviews back to back? He shared that after several interviews he has come to an understanding of the basic questions those are asked by the evaluator on his Technology. That is absolutely true. Most of the time you would find 90% of the questions are repeated. It's not all your interviewers are copying it from Google but still the basics of any technology is not going to change so there could be variations but more or less you would find the questions - repeated. It is always going to be helpful to browse through Google and prepare common interview questions for your domain. Please see, my intention is not to ask you to just limit yourself to these questions but it is must do - to ensure that you do not stumble upon the very basic questions which 90% of the audience would be able to answer. Another important skill set to have is to ensure that you know your current process Inside Out. At times a person is not very well versed with the complete gamut of services provided by a particular technology or application but as long as an individual is able to elaborate and detail out what he does in day to day affairs, such person can also be considered. However, if you know the technology Inside Out but you are not able to elaborate on what you do on a day to day basis there could be a perception that you are not focused in your work and that doesn't go well with the interviewers so the trick here is to do the following:

- Read from google what are the most frequently asked questions for your domain.

- Revise the entire process and revisit your day today work to ensure you are able to advise your daily job with absolute details.

- In case you are applying for a management position definitely ensure that you are on top of your metrics and how have you been doing on those parameters off late.

Preparation is key

Most of the questions would be situation based and you will be better served if you quote examples from your experience. Instead of answering "I believe this should be done"/ "I think this should have been done or should be done" - Instead "In past this is what I did and following were my outcomes" That make you sound authentic and experienced - earlier statements are more of a cacophony.

Do not speak more than necessary or asked for.

Interview is not over till you have joined.:) Ensure do not drop your guard till you are selected. At times interviewers would come across as so simple and easy going, where you tend to open up more than you should and at times you end up exposing more than necessary.

Positive Conditioning of Mind: Ensure you read Rhonda Byrne - Secret - if you have even slight belief in omens. Imagine the positive outcome all the way till you get the job. That definitely kicks in your confidence. Under confidence is the worst deterrent.

How to crack interviews?

This is an interesting question. Everyone wants to know the answer to this question but let me tell you that no shoe fits all. What might have worked for one person may not work for another because every interview is unique. Still if I have to drill down to the basics which if not hundred percent of situations but at least majority of situations would help you to sail through.

Be truthful and your natural self

This my first and foremost tip to you. This has been invariably the most effective thing I could advise for clearing the interviews. The more you try to pretend, the more chances for your failure. In case you feel that you would have to pretend a lot to clear this interview you are really not applying for the right kind of role and even if you get through the interview, you are going to eventually lose out and end up suffering in the job. Once you decide to be yourself, your natural self, you automatically get a lot of confidence and that reflects in your overall body language, tone and answers so please do not try to be someone else just be yourself and enjoy the experience. Have a candid and sensible conversation - the chances for success would increase manifold.

You would have done it all

In case you are not a fresher – after 3 to 4 years of experience you would have mostly gone through the complete cycle of what is expected of you in your next job so just learn to present it properly - be able to relate to competencies.

Let's say there is an opening for knowledge base & process management manager and you have always been a Service Delivery guy a Service Delivery Manager. now there is no direct mapping in the roles that you are applying for and what you are doing currently. Think again and you would realise at some point of time you would have really worked on knowledge management in some capacity. Maybe during an initiative for a project or just an informal request or maybe just for the development of a team. In the interview you have to highlight your competency about this. You need to muster all the knowledge that you have accumulated while working on that knowledge management work and I am sure you would be able to do this role. After completion of a few years in an organisation especially at a management level, you could rest assured that you would have got experience with everything, maybe to varying degrees based on the organisation and your participation. So the important point here is to focus on your experience with the lens of the new organisation's requirement. Once you focus on finding a relevant experience from your day to day life you will be able to find that at some point you would have done the required role and you would be able to deliver in the new org as well.

Energy Levels/Confidence/Ease and Humour

Nothing beats the energy levels, confidence and humour (right quantity). In case you are not feeling well please do not turn up for interview it's OK to get it rescheduled but ensure that you are at your best while you're sitting in front of the panel. There are some people who are by nature very passive and there are few people who are by nature very aggressive and they have their respective energy levels accordingly. There is something surreal which happens at a subconscious level. Let's say you are the hiring manager and you are by nature an aggressive personality and the person who is sitting in front of you is very laid back, lacking energy so he may be fit for the purpose but chances of him getting through would reduce significantly and vice versa. In my opinion an aggressive person can go slow and match energy levels of the panel if its low while for a passive or low energy level individual, he would have to struggle to go to higher energy levels because it will not be his or her natural self and potentially may not look very good. I've also found that generally the people with aggression, will to kill and high level of energy levels generally make through most of the interviews when compared to people with less energy. My earnest request to you, you may usually prefer to be a very quiet and silent person but at least demonstrate certain level of energy, enthusiasm, so that the hiring individual realises that you would be able to do the job.

Match the energy levels and just be yourself don't look too professional or overstressed just go with the flow and you should be ok.

Please be very careful with the humour I am sure we all are grown up and understand how sensitive inappropriate humour could be so be humorous only when you are sure you're not hurting someone, you are not showing down someone and it's not political or driven by any other bias or prejudice.

Dressing

Recently I was interviewing someone that turned up with a shirt hanging out, in the floaters (footwear) and shirt was also not ironed. He even didn't look like taken shower. To my surprise he has come from home not directly from office. Right in the morning and was going to his office in the same outfit. He was anyways average technically and not presentable. You would always like to hire someone who is presentable and can be sent to customer meetings without any fear of misrepresentation. Maybe I was old school but I think the majority of people get in the hiring positions are old school so this kind of new generation clothing may not fly every time. I have met some brilliant people who came in jeans and shirt and we hired them but it's not always the case. It's better to keep it to optimum to ensure that you do not attract negative points just by dressing. The mantra here's to look your best and to keep it appropriate with the new organisation. if required do some research - let me reiterate that keeping this standard clothing would be better than taking chances with more adventurous clothing for interviews.

These days going with formal coat/jacket is also not always positive so keep it simple, see if you can get some insider information of what would be more acceptable - formal shirt and pants or simple business casuals should do the trick

Idea here is "Look your best – be your best!"

Body Language

Already covered the body language but here I would like to stress one important point that some people are now well versed with the body language basics and thus please be mindful of the following:

- *Itching Nose:* While talking do not tell many lies because if you tell lies you would mostly have an itchy nose. Maybe some uncomfortable sensation in your face where you would be bringing your hands up to cover your face or mouth or to itch your nose. They are an indicator of you being not as honest as the interviewer would like you to be. Try it for yourself, nose usually itches whenever you try to tell something that was not hundred percent true.

- *Gaze:* Secondly be careful of in which direction you are looking at while answering. When someone is cooking up stories the person would usually look up towards his Right so if your interviewer knows this - you are anyways in a fix. Figure for reference. Try it yourself:)

Below picture is to be viewed as person sitting infront of you.

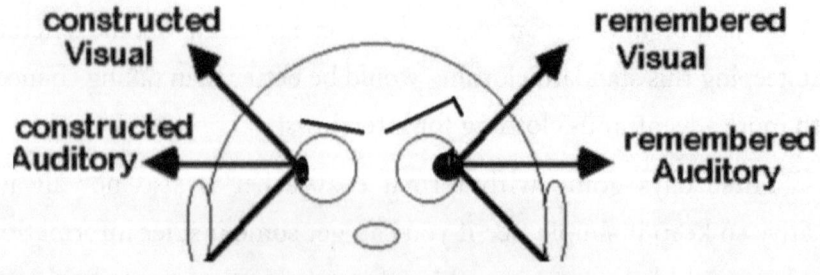

which means – if he/she looks at "your right" – "its remembered or recalled – hence true"

Listen – Pause – Answer

Listening properly and Thinking before you answer is key. Sometime ago we rejected a person not just because of this but yes this also was one of the contributing factors. Whenever we were asking him a question the answer was not very straight forward. We had to ask and repeat ourselves several times to get what we were looking forward to. There is no problem for me to ask him the question as many times as I want because we are sitting at a leisure and the only thing you have to do is this conversation but when there is a crisis at work and you happen to interact with this kind of person on floor it would be a menace. Updates would not be straight forward and such confusing statements or beating around the bush can cost you several minutes and create lot of frustration. We may not even realise how this small thing can lead up to business impact and that is why one of the reasons for selection and rejection. Kindly keep it crisp and to the point. In order to achieve this you would have to listen properly, plan your answer and then only convey with your words.

Positive about your previous org, team and Management

This is an interesting and very important point. Do not use interview as a forum to vent out your frustrations and how bad your previous company was. Nobody wants to connect with a sucker or a cribber. It reflects badly on you because hiring manager could deduce that today you are cribbing about your previous company and tomorrow you would be crying about my company because it's in your attitude and trust me you could be outrightly rejected.

Keep your emotions and sentiments about your previous organisation to yourself as its none of their concern and even the hiring manager won't be able to make any difference in your previous organisation so no point in being a cribber. However I would encourage you to *talk very high and positive about your existing company* that demonstrates your maturity and positivity.

Salary Expectations

Try to not to tell salary expectation upfront - unless you are through to HR round or know your walk away amount:

This is just to ensure that you do not go unrealistic with demand which is way out of bounds for the hiring company. By the time you reach the HR round you have got a reasonable clarity about what to expect from the organisation and at the same time organisation has also made up its mind whether you are fit for the position or not and that is a nice time to decide whether you want to go ahead or not and at the same time organisations can also evaluate your ask against your performance. Recommendation would be to keep this discussion as a last thing and during the conversation you can maintain that money won't be a deal breaker as long as we are following the company standards. This also conveys that you are not just behind the money while you're making the change but at times interviewer would like you to really advise - in that case go ahead and advise.

Ensure you find out - what is industry standard for such positions.

Flexibility

While hiring in almost every interview that I have taken, I have been very particular about the flexibility of the candidate. Even if the role may not demand that level of flexibility but I want to ensure that the person I'm hiring is capable of working in difficult situations and be able to manage the stress that at times come along with the inhuman shifts and more than 7 days of work week. It's another must have rather than a good to have quality in the person you're hiring. I am not asking you to befool the interview panel by saying that I have/would be available 24 x 7 instead make up your mind that now the organisations have shaped up in a way that 24 x 7 shift has pretty much become a norm. In case you are not already working in 24 x 7 shift good for you but always be open that the next job might need you to work in 24x7 setup. It is especially required when you are supporting customers in time zones other than yours. In case your new job asks you for a night shift and you have not been used to of night shifts I would strongly recommend to try maybe a small project or something in the existing organisation where you work few nights just to get a sense of it. Do not sign for a night shift until unless you are really comfortable with them.

Challenges & Conflict Management

This is an interesting set of questions I have combined in one. You would invariably be evaluated on your ability to manage stress, challenges and conflicts. This gets spicy when you are asked to quote examples like - Quote an example when you had a conflict with your Boss. The reason is not that they are interested in this story that you are telling but what they are looking forward to is what approach you have taken.

There was an interview where I have almost finalized a gentleman and was having a casual chit chat I asked him if at any point of time he had a conflict with his manager. For some reason he went on saying that he is never bothered about his manager, he never cares, he does what he believes is right and at times he went back and told his manager that I would do what I want to do and I will not listen to your bullshit. He wasn't selected. These questions help the hiring manager to evaluate your maturity and how would you respond if you are put or subjected to a similar situation and in your new organisation so please be very careful. Do not show off, how strong you have been while fighting with your colleagues and managers. All the challenges and conflicts have to be resolved amicably and with facts and figures.

Know industry and company you are giving interview for

I won't say that if you don't know much about your industry you would not be selected in interviews. For entry level positions it won't really matter but from mid-level management I strongly urge you to read and make yourself well versed with your industry. You shall keep an eye on all the new emerging trends. Not just with your organisation but also with the industry in general and also know as much as you could find about your new organisation. This question becomes much more important when you are going from a big brand to a smaller brand. People grill you really hard if you are going to a company which is lesser known because of two reasons - one, either because of curiosity that why you are sacrificing a big brand for a smaller one and secondly, they want to explore if you would really be serious if you join the organisation. While answering this question if you are able to provide facts and figures about this smaller organisation what great things they have accomplished in so less time than your chances of getting through this question are much higher otherwise the interviewer would take it for granted that you are just making a change because of better package or problem in your current org and you care less about where you are getting in to. Doesn't look like someone who makes very informed decisions.

Chapter 9

SOCIAL MEDIA MANAGEMENT

Nowadays people would believe what they see about you on Facebook and Instagram than what you would tell them on their face. LinkedIn especially has been used profoundly to do hiring and also people can make perceptions about you based on what they see about you on any of these social media applications or website. Most of the time before anybody hires you, people generally review your profile, if available on LinkedIn and now people at times evaluate your excursions on Facebook as well. I don't say that's fair or even ethical to do it but I know people who do it. I was surprised myself once I found one of my senior managers who shared a feedback about a person by sheer looking at persons profile on Facebook. Very soon we realised that he was right.

Now this is going to be a little overboard - to insure sanity- what I am going to tell you, you may not like because then you would lose your freedom of what you post on LinkedIn, WhatsApp and Facebook.

Thus any comment that you make has to be evaluated especially if its related to your organization or to someone to whom team may be able to relate to.

Let's say you are a CEO of a company and your WHATSAPP status reads "Seriously Sad and disappointed" - you may be feeling sad may be because of something negligibly small but think tanks would go berserk and start making their own interpretation of what may have gone wrong. In the worst case, even your share price may come down just because you posted something like this. I know what I am saying here is far from reality but this exaggeration is just to ensure that we understand that you are monitored. Even at a simple leadership position also if you make a statement like "even when I am kidding I am not kidding" your team members might get a very different message so the sooner you climb up the ladder you have to start getting more and more careful about your interactions with the individuals and more importantly how you demonstrate yourself over any of these social media applications. I don't say these applications are bad or detrimental but have to be used with caution. There are several advantages as well that you can leverage for various things.

LinkedIn

In today's world if you are a professional you should really have a great online presence in case you want to do better in life and professionally. Some good practices which have observed in LinkedIn are as follows

1. Keep your profile up to date.
2. Feel free to flaunt your accomplishments – Certifications, recognitions, references etc.
3. Republish or share your organisation's success stories.
4. Avoid unnecessary confrontations, take them offline if unavoidable.
5. Do follow some of the experts in your domain and some leaders who can help u shape your own thought process.

WhatsApp

WhatsApp is now a medium to share content within your team members so keep it natural don't press so hard but just ensure that you do not share things which are demotivating in nature and which make fun of your current organisation. Especially if your boss is there just ensure that you maintain the dignity of the position while you are posting. I would strongly recommend to avoid sharing jokes which are associated to Boss because not all the bosses are very sporting with jokes. At any point of time you get some good information about the organisation which is praise worthy please feel free to share that. It serves two purposes one it shows that you are happy with your organisation and secondly it helps to reinforce positivity among the team members also about the organisation. Any bit of positivity that you can contribute to the overall environment is worth every effort it takes.

Try to have a separate WhatsApp number and do not share with your org or customers unless you are really comfortable with them. In your WhatsApp status you may want to go crazy but let's say you are at a very senior position - it may not go well with everyone. Please be mindful of what you post as your team as well as your manager might have a look at it and unintentionally you maybe just creating curiosity and unnecessarily spreading the fire which may not be worth the time and efforts.

Facebook

You like it or you don't like it but if you are on Facebook your personal life is on display definitely depending on how much you have put on the showcase so in case you want your personal life to be kept really personal please change the settings of Facebook or else be open with the fact that anything and everything that you are posting is being read by your office colleagues, your management and your new hiring manager as well. Anything that you feel would be helpful in all aspects for all these stakeholders feel free to post but in case you see some of them may be counterproductive then please do not post such content on your Facebook page.

Not what you post on your Facebook page matters but where you are tagged also does matter. Until you are sure that you have a great relationship with an individual please do not accept his or her friend request and give tagging permission. Please see this note was not to deter you from using FB but the idea is to ensure you have a sensitivity around your image and anything online is available for everyone's consumption…!

Chapter 10

PROFESSIONAL NETWORKING

Now the time has come when you have put down your paper moving to a different business, different organisation all goods and bads of this current organisation would cease to matter to a large extent. This is an exciting feeling and makes you feel very light hearted. Especially the farewells are the interesting parts because you get to hear so many good things about you and gradually you shake hands even with your not so good friends and depart. Just slow down the process and let's review some of the important aspects while you are on your way out and how can you make this time matter for your long term success.

Please note that the organisation you are leaving behind was made up of people and this is a small world.. very often roads would cross some people who are reporting into you might become manager and some of your managers might be reporting to you in future. No one knows. Do use this time to forge some strong bond with your existing team or at least ensure you are leaving the team and most of them on talking terms - the departing team.

Importance of peer network

The rapport, relationship with your previous and current colleagues is important as it shapes up your peer network. This peer network goes a long way - at least in my last 4 offer letters - I got them as someone has referred me, those peers, colleagues, friends may not take your interview but they can make you feel a "lesser" stranger - while hiring manager is head hunting the strangers. This gives a great starting point to you while preparing for the job and also to the hiring manager - it's a win - win.

In today's connected world this goes a long way. Your good and bad feedback travels miles without you even being aware of it. I can tell you multiple situations where people who may not even know that I have contributed to their success or a failure in an interview. Referral plays a very important role in the current world and especially for the senior positions generally people prefer to hire somebody known than a complete stranger. The devil you know is better than the devil you don't so anytime in future whenever you start looking forward for a change of job you would invariably turn back to these team members and maybe from your previous organisations as well to get recommendations and opportunity so keep this relationship going and do not burn bridges and forget. Keep in touch once in a while to ensure that if you really need someone's help you don't have to bother with thought of "Friends with benefits" be a genuine friend - try to help your friends and peers as much as you could so that help comes handy when you need it.

Keeping the line open/Not burn the bridges it's a small world

In order to keep the conversation going on you can use social media. May create a group on WhatsApp or occasionally send a broadcast. Wishing Birthdays/Anniversaries is also a great opportunity to keep in touch. Don't do this for the sake of job and purpose - but deeply love people who stood by you during some challenging times and just show respect to such moments by keeping the connection alive.

Helping the peers to get help if required

Before you can ask for help you rather be helping others. In case at any given point of time you get request by someone looking for a job or any help please do your level best to help. It goes a long way. It gives you a great satisfaction if you are able to help somebody get a good job and you never know when such favour is returned. It will make a great difference if God forbade you are in need of help. Always believe this kind of teamwork and selfless support to your peers and previous team members can go a long way In making everybody's life better in terms of career.

Chapter 11

EXITS

Before your last day or on your last day you are ready to pack up that box and leave. This is an important phase of your career. This is like a last portion of your movie. How would you feel if you were watching a movie where entire movie was good but towards the end they screwed up the plot. Made it bad enough that you may not even want to recommend it to anyone or say - you can just go for the first half of the movie and then please leave by the interval.

Same happens to us as individuals. It's a small world and you never know when you will be working or reporting to the same set of people at some point in the future. That means when you have done so much of hard work to ensure that you are in the good books of everyone then why to lose that by not acting well during your exits. With that said, let me share a story one of our friends Santosh while he was leaving the organisation he continued to work brilliantly as always till his last working day. He went the extra mile capturing all details that may be required by the team behind him. Documented everything neat and tidy. Structured the stuff before he left.

He impressed everyone so much that as soon as we got another opportunity we hired him back with a better package I assume (He didn't give party:P). It always pays to not to burn the bridges and ensure that you do not screw up your performance just because you are now on your way out.

Let's Explore few of the options that would help us to ensure we have got it right.

Clean up your tasks

Review your work completely and ensure any pending or half-baked work is also completed to its best and you are not leaving anything unfinished at your end. Think from the perspective of what all things may become a problem for other team members once you are out of the organisation. Please complete them to the logical conclusion and handover all the details to someone who can take it forward in your absence.

Documentation

Please document all the work that you have done. create SOP or a standard operational process for doing all the things that you are doing. There should be a very detailed information of each and every role and responsibility that you are doing and also list down any best practices that you might have developed/evolved during the course of your duties within the organization.

Show maturity and appreciation for existing team

While you are on your way out don't use this time to share all the secrets you have accumulated all these years and use them against all your so called enemies within the org. You are leaving but others have to stay and still work together. Your small comments and misadventure can spoil the environment of the team and render irreparable loss to the organisation. Instead use this time to thank people who have been helpful to you. It would be great if you could share some real life examples of how somebody has made a meaningful contribution to your career or work. Gratitude would never go out of fashion. There might be a few people with whom you did not get along very well so for them you can keep just professional thanks and leave it there.

No hard feelings

How inconsequential this may sound but this statement is very powerful. Take a deep breath smile and address the whole team. Say that they might have been some good and some not so good experiences with each other but while I move on I would like to apologize for any wrong that might have happened knowingly or unknowingly and make a statement.

> *"No hard feelings, we end here all not so great things & feelings - here onwards we are just one thing, if not more - friends."*

I am sure you would come up with your own set of the statements But please have a carefully crafted statement that fits your team and also goes well with your own value system. I am not insisting or forcing here to bend down to a level where you do not like it but please ensure that you give your best shot to clear up anything that anybody might have against you. It's a small world and you never know you may be working with whom and in what capacity thus it's never a good idea to leave with enemies behind and it just don't make sense so let's be more mature and resolve any such issues.

Happy to hire you back

Notice period is a very interesting period. majority of people get casual at this juncture when you have an offer in hand. Existing company start looking useless and you tend to take the company for granted. Ignoring the fact that for all the days you are going to work in the organisation during your notice period you would also be paid by the existing company. Professionally we should respect the matter that you are still being paid for these days and you are answerable to your work and office accordingly. Thus you should ensure that you give your best and even more during your last few days within the organisation.

"We are good as our last transaction"

My manager and coach Sameer introduced me to this statement ☺ so identify the opportunities or create few last good interactions to ensure that people are appreciative of your work and all bid adieu to you in great spirits.

Chapter 12

JOB IS NOT LIFE

While I come to the closure of this book I have tried to share all what you can do to be a top performer in your organisation based on observations - this is not Bible or Geeta or the book of truth but experience. You would have to play with these ideas, observe in your team, other teams, peers from current and last companies and make up your own mind - This book is sure to deliver results.

However, I can assure, this book is a great place to begin your journey of being a top performer. This book outlines practical insights to management view of employees. How you can rise beyond common and make your mark.

Whatever is listed here is what most of us have realized with experience, you would also realize it yourself once you reach that level in the organisation.

Family and Work have to be balanced

Work is just work at the end of the day. In case you get permanently disabled or critically ill - who would take care of you?? Boss, Colleagues or HR or Customer? Would there be a salary if you don't work the answer is brutal and the answer is **NO**. Then who would help or take care of you? Family and Friends - Right?

So you need to strike the balance - Focus on your work but do not compromise your family completely. Especially when they need you. Feel free to talk to your manager and Boss figure out the way for work life balance. I am not advocating that you become careless and take ad-hoc leave all the time but do ensure that like your work priorities your home is also a Priority and people at your home are well taken care of.

Nothing would matter once you are out

Whatever is causing the stress in your work life, may be a failure to meet a deadline, a clumsy project/product that you delivered, missed office sales target, you might be spending sleepless night for it today but do you think it would matter tomorrow? Try to reflect, if you have changed your company anytime in the past and try to recall if any of those failures matter to you today? There might have been disasters, delivered extremely useless product/software and or have done outages - does it matter now? My intention here is not to promote carelessness and lackadaisical approach but what I really want to ensure that you are not taking yourself or your family members for granted because of something that has not gone the way you wanted to go in the organisation to kill you. Take a deep breath and do your best. Don't intentionally screw up things, plan properly and execute well but still in case things don't go well do not kill yourself.

Challenges only make you

"That doesn't kill you, makes you stronger."

If you ask anyone who has been in the corporate for some time he or she can clearly tell you that they would have got the most important lessons only during failures.

Resilience- Setbacks and failures are part of life, but how you choose to deal with those roadblocks is what critical to your success	Madhup Nagpal

No one learns while living in the comfortable running operations and systems. So whenever you are going through tough time rest assured that you would remember that time and share the stories of the same time over and over again in future. Whenever somebody's calling you for an issue or asking you to help him during an issue please do not hesitate. Always consider this as a learning opportunity and after sometime these challenges would be business as usual for you but for others it will be a miracle the way you would be able to manage these situations. Such expertise and disaster management skills would ensure you as the top performer for years to come.

Be passionate and make time for family and yourself

I briefly talked about this but I would like to insist that you should never ever compromise your family or your health. "Health is wealth" is an old saying but very true so never ever underestimate your health and take good care of yourself. It's like a refilling station - If you have to reach somewhere quickly, you can't ignore the need of petrol or gas so while you are running fast on the road of your career and you want to speed it up, you would fail miserably if you have completely ignored your health and family.

Now the Most Important Quote -

Performance measurement is relative in corporate world. Stop trying to be a top performer. because you are limiting yourself and your potential to that of your peers with whom the performance calibration is done. That's why Lot of top companies having great people practice are moving away from performance rating and calibration. Instead focus on your core strength what is unique about you how you can harness that to create/deliver tangible business value and outcome.. remember everyone is born unique, one can't ask an eagle to swim nor a fish to fly. So find your purpose, focus on the process and make sure you do the right thing, result and outcome that defines the performance will be a by-product of the process. So what you do every day is important	Adarsh Mudugere

Thanks for picking up this book and I am sure if you have come this far to complete this book you will go places in your career as well.

Wishing you again – great success, health, wealth and amazing life ahead! Good Luck!

Yours

– Prashant Dixit

I would be happy to hear back from you and answer any queries that you might have.

In case you are interested in personal coaching you can connect with us at.

Email: prashant.dixit.win@gmail.com
Facebook: prashant.dixit.win
Twitter: @prashant_dixit_
Instagram: @iprashantdixit
Website: www.prashantdixit.in

NOTE FOR READERS

We have taken inputs from leaders and have compiled them as per theme of the book. None of the leader directly or indirectly endorses these interpretations. Whatever is written here are author's interpretation except for quotes those are directly provided by the leaders they all are written with their names. The information shared in this work is more of a suggestive literature please use your discretion as mentioned earlier. No one associated with this work can be held responsible for any damage, loss or whatsoever. Author doesn't take any responsibility of any unwanted outcome and can't be challenged legally or otherwise. Readers to use their discretion.

APPENDIX 1

S No	In order of reporting year 2006 to 2020
1	Senthil
2	Suman
3	Madan
4	David
5	Ananathan
6	Meenal
7	Archana
8	Adarsh
9	Vijay Krishnan
10	Sitaram
11	Madhup
12	Hafiz
13	Adarsh

14	Brent
15	Sameer
16	Sudhindra
17	Ambrish
18	Matt Stramel
19	Matt Lindeman
20	James Jaconetti

APPENDIX 2 – EXTRA STUFF

Link for Power Dressing:

https://www.thehrdigest.com/power-power-dressing/

Outlook Rule to Delay Email:

To configure delay in Outlook for outbox.

You can alternately search for following on Google "Delay the delivery of all messages"

https://support.office.com/en-us/article/delay-or-schedule-sending-email-messages-026af69f-c287-490a-a72f-6c65793744ba

APPENDIX 3 – RESEARCH DETAILS

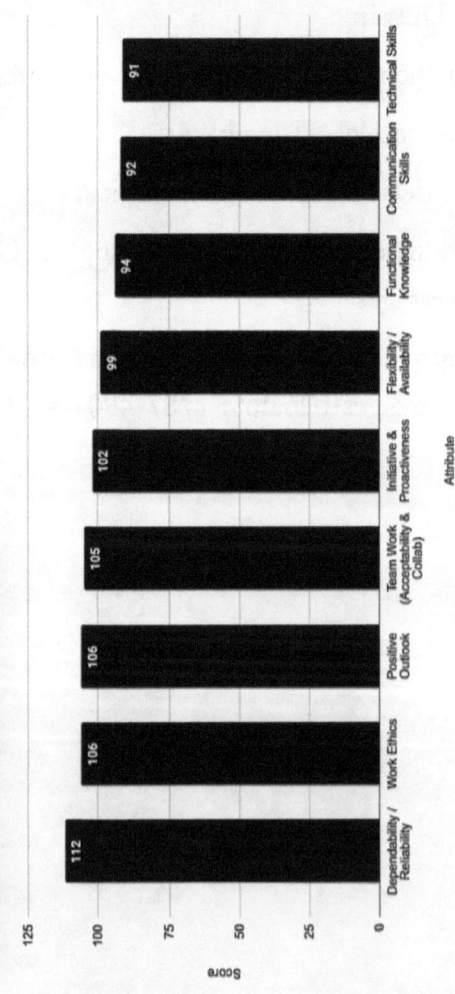

Appendix 3 – Research Details

Leader	Current Company	Designation	Functional Knowledge - What and Why of things.	Technical Skills - How of things	Flexibility / Availability: How much person is flexible or available during business exigencies	Team Work (Acceptability & Collab): Does person takes the team along. Is he/she is Go to Guy for Team & manager	Dependabilit y / Reliability: Person can be trusted for critical projects and difficult situations	Initiative & Proactiv eness	Communicati on Skills	Work Ethics - Need no follow ups, self driven high quality standards, punctuality and team process adherence	Positive Outlook: Is mostly positive in action and thoughts. Doesn't crib & complain instead focuses on solutions.	Total Experien ce (Years)	Years of Experien ce in Perform ance Reviews
Ambrish Sharma	Cisco Systems	Services Delivery Manager	9	9	10	10	10	10	8	10	10	20	15
Anantha Amancharla	SS&C	Director	10	9	10	10	10	8	9	9	9	21	17
Wasi abidi	Mondelz international	Global head Delivery DWP	7	8	10	10	10	9	8	10	10	20	15
Uttam Banerjee	Ekam Eco Solutions	CEO	9	7	9	10	9	10	6	9	10	14	9
Sameer Srivastava	Mytel	Director	9	7	8	9	10	8	8	9	10	21	14
Murali Nayak	Veritas Technologies	Director	7	7	8	9	9	9	9	10	10	22	15
Anurag Bahadur	Cisco	Senior Director	8	8	9	9	10	9	7	9	9	21	15
Adarsh Mudugere	VMware	Director - CXS	9	8	6	9	10	10	7	9	9	20	14
Matthew Stramel	Zscaler	Sr. Director of Professional Services	7	8	7	6	7	6	9	9	10	20	10
Sameer Bondre	Kohler	Director	8	7	6	5	10	8	7	9	8	18	12
Madhup Nagpal	Druva	Vice President	5	7	7	8	7	10	9	6	6	15	8
Ravi Mylariah	Teknodreams software	VP Delivery	6	6	9	10	10	5	5	7	5	32	20

Appendix 3 – Research Details

Research was done with Leaders who have worked in the industry and have done reasonably well in their career. These all bring lot of leadership expertise that can guide the folks in their career.

Process: Interviews were conducted for few leaders and for few leaders a survey was rolled out and feedback received. Then compilation was done.

Thanks to all the leaders who contributed to this project! Below is the table that represents their experience in performance management and overall. Each year we all learn something new and we are more experienced as life & work keep on teaching us one thing or the other.

We would never be able to experience all the learnings world and work has to offer by ourselves and thus learning from each other does matter and helps us all to get better.

If you and I share what you and I know – we together get insights and advantage of cumulative experience.

Similarly – what these all leaders learnt by themselves, from their leaders, colleagues etc – by talking to them, taking their feedback and inputs – I am happy to share that we are looking at cumulative experience of 325 years!! From leaders, if there experience is put together – its more than 200! years in performance management… This amount of experience we can't earn in our single life time! So far a human limitation. ☺

Thanks to all the **leaders!**

Appendix 3 – Research Details

Name	Org	Designation	Total Experience (Years)	Years of Experience in Performance Reviews
Adarsh Mudugere	VMware	Director	20	14
Ajay Sharma	Cisco	Services Delivery Manager	22	15
Ambrish Sharma	Cisco Systems	Services Delivery Manager	20	15
Anantha Amancharla	SS&C	Director	21	17
Anurag Bahadur	Cisco	Senior Director	21	15
Geral Wislon	Vodafone Idea	Vice President	24	10
Krishna Pandey	NICE	Director	22	15
Madhup Nagpal	Druva	Vice President	15	8
Matthew Stramel	Zscaler	Senior Director	20	10
Murrali Nayak	Veritas Technologies	Director	22	15
Prashant Dixit	Druva	Senior Manager	13	7
Ravi Mylariah	Teknodreams software	Vice President	32	20
Sameer Bondre	Kohler	Director	18	12
Sameer Srivastava	Mytel	Director	21	14
Uttam Banerjee	Ekam Eco Solutions	CEO	14	9
Wasi Abidi	Mondelz International	Global Head Delivery(DWP)	20	15
		Total Years	**325**	**211**

183

APPENDIX 4

My story

While I was new to the corporate world - I was focussed on joining IIMs and never took my day job seriously. Lack of focus landed me into being a Poor Performer in my first project. I was everything but a software developer. I was not useless though, as I was still heading TCS Studio in Karapakkam Chennai office, part of Toastmasters club there, head of canteen committee and contributed to CSR activities of TCS. While I was a known figure outside my project, my managers were surely not impressed and I paid the price. I was rated Low. Then I took transfer to Mumbai for some personal reasons and landed into a project at TCS Jogeshwari-Mumbai which was already struggling with deadlines. By then I already had my CAT score - 92 percentile - not sufficient to get into IIM so parked CAT for a while and focussed on Project. It was the first time I made some significant contribution and project was completed as expected. After this project I was sent to Thane office of TCS where I actually learnt and grew technically and in 2009 joined AVAYA - By this time I had changed as a person and have become a dependable resource. Since then till now - have never looked back and have augmented responsibilities beyond my years of experience. I truly enjoy my work and challenges I get to work on during my day to day work. While I traversed through this journey whatever I have learnt - I would share and I am confident you will benefit with exp**eriences shared here.**

Good Luck!!

www.ingramcontent.com/pod-product-compliance
Lightning Source LLC
Chambersburg PA
CBHW020909180526
45163CB00007B/2674